CONTENTS

D1495161

INTRODUCTION BY JUDGE CATHERINE McGUINNESS,   1
CHAIRPERSON OF THE FORUM FOR PEACE AND RECONCILIATION

PAPERS ON
THE NATURE OF THE PROBLEM AND THE
PRINCIPLES UNDERLYING ITS RESOLUTION   5

1.   Fianna Fáil   7
2.   Social Democratic and Labour Party   11
3.   Fine Gael   19
4.   Labour Party   25
5.   Sinn Féin   35
6.   Progressive Democrats   41
7.   Alliance Party   49
8.   Democratic Left   55
9.   Senator Gordon Wilson   65
10. The Green Party/An Comhaontas Glas   73
11. Independent Deputies   85
12. Independent Senators   89
13. The Workers' Party   91

RESPONSES TO
A NEW FRAMEWORK FOR AGREEMENT   97

1.   Fianna Fáil   99
2.   Social Democratic and Labour Party   103
3.   Fine Gael   107
4.   Labour Party   111
5.   Sinn Féin   115
6.   Progressive Democrats   119

7.	Alliance Party	125
8.	Democratic Left	129
9.	Senator Gordon Wilson	133
10.	The Green Party/An Comhaontas Glas	135
11.	Independent Deputies	137
12.	Independent Senators	141
13.	The Workers' Party	145

Terms of Reference of the Forum   149

List of Speakers   151

INTRODUCTION

THE FORUM FOR PEACE AND RECONCILIATION was established on foot of an undertaking made in the Joint Declaration of December 1993 to enable democratic Parties 'to consult together and share in dialogue about the political future'. It was envisaged that the Forum would make recommendations 'on ways in which agreement and trust between both traditions can be promoted and established'. With this objective in mind, every political Party in Ireland with a democratic mandate was invited to participate and, in all, thirteen Delegations took up this offer.

The Forum's terms of reference made it quite clear that participation was without prejudice to the positions held by its members on constitutional questions. No Party was being asked to leave its constitutional aspirations behind at the door of the Forum. On the contrary, there was a desire to listen to the full range of views represented by the political Parties on the island. The only entry requirement was a firm commitment to resolving political differences by exclusively peaceful and democratic means.

With its terms of reference agreed by the participating Delegations, the Forum opened its doors on 28 October 1994 when its inaugural session was held in St Patrick's Hall at Dublin Castle. The Parties involved knew from the outset that the Forum was not intended to be, nor could it become, a formal negotiating arena. However, in the climate of peace brought about by the paramilitary ceasefires, there was an obvious need for a venue where political leaders could explore the many issues pertinent to the achievement of a durable political agreement acceptable to all the parties to the conflict. The Forum was conceived as a venue where this essential talking could take place and it has already served that function well.

After its opening session, the Forum agreed a work programme which highlighted a number of specific themes such as: the Economic Consequences of Peace; Parity of Esteem; Fundamental Rights and Freedoms; Justice Issues; Obstacles in the South to Reconciliation; North-South Co-operation; and Constitutional Questions and Political Structures. Over the months, the Forum has delved into all of these issues and encouraged the Delegations to think about them afresh in the new and positive setting arising out of the ceasefires.

Aside from these topics, the Forum saw a need, as a basis for its further work, to conduct a careful analysis of the nature of the problem with a view to identifying those principles relevant to the growth of a political settlement. Each Delegation was asked to reflect on this issue and thirteen policy papers were submitted which outline their basic thinking on how the conflict in Northern Ireland can be resolved. These papers, which form the core of this book, were presented to the Forum over a two month period and are now being compiled as a contribution to a better understanding of how the Forum Delegations view the future of Ireland. As part of the Forum's debates, each paper was subjected to an intensive scrutiny by the other Delegations which required the Parties to defend, and elaborate on, their thinking. This turned out to be a very productive exercise which highlighted the value of an open and inclusive political dialogue.

Our purpose in collecting these papers into a single volume is to draw attention to the rich complexity of political opinion they embody. It is hoped that this publication will allow the different views of the Forum Delegations to reach a wider audience, especially in Northern Ireland. The Forum is founded on the premise that dialogue, even between those who disagree in fundamental ways, can serve to clarify issues and promote better understanding. It is only by achieving an improved mutual understanding that our island's divided traditions can reach the accommodation needed to secure a peaceful future for all the people of Ireland.

The second section of this book assembles the views of the Forum Delegations in response to A New Framework for Agreement to which, in view of its central importance in the development of the peace process, the Forum has devoted considerable attention since its publication. The Delegations outlined their initial positions on A New Framework for Agreement at a meeting of the Forum on 3 March 1995 and a number of subsequent meetings have been devoted to examining its principal features.

When the Framework Document appeared, I made the point, in welcoming its publication, that the work of the Forum is suffused with the spirit of the Joint Declaration whose guiding principles — self-determination, the freely-given consent of the governed, commitment to exclusively democratic and peaceful means, full respect and protection for the rights and identities of both traditions - also explicitly form the basis of the Framework Document. Given the power and wide appeal of these principles, I would urge all those with an interest in creating a peaceful, tolerant, and prosperous Ireland, both North and South, to be prepared to talk to one another – whatever they may think of the detail of the Framework Document itself. It seems to me that the Forum's experience has shown that nobody has anything to fear, and everybody has much to gain, from frank, open and inclusive dialogue.

Having presided over the Forum's weekly meetings since October 1994, I have been impressed by its success in stimulating dialogue between Parties with deep political differences, some of whom are encountering each other for the first time in this manner. This experience, and the frankness of its exchanges which have, I might add, been conducted in a highly constructive atmosphere, encourage me to believe that the wider, and more difficult, dialogue that needs to take place with the involvement of the Unionist Parties can ultimately also be a fruitful one. The Forum remains available as a place where the Unionist Parties can, if they so wish, come to debate the key issues of the peace process outside the confines of an actual negotiating environment. Although I regret the absence from the Forum of the mainstream Unionist Parties, I have been struck by the very strong evidence of a genuine desire on the part of Forum Delegations to take account of unionist concerns. Indeed, it is widely felt among Forum members that the sessions, notably those addressed by the Protestant

Churches, at which unionist concerns have been voiced have been among the most powerful we have had. The Forum is equally keen to give a voice to the concerns of nationalists in Northern Ireland, as these are not always fully understood in the South. All in all, the Forum has devoted a great deal of time to listening to the views of those outside the political Parties (including business groups, trade unions, farmers' organisations, the voluntary and community sectors and victims of violence) with something to contribute to a better understanding of the conflict and its potential remedies.

Even without mainstream Unionist involvement, I remain convinced that the Forum can perform a valuable function as a testing ground for the new concepts and arrangements required to convert the peace we now enjoy into the durable political settlement we all desire.

JUDGE CATHERINE McGUINNESS

The
NATURE *of the* PROBLEM
and the
PRINCIPLES UNDERLYING
ITS RESOLUTION

POLICY PAPERS BY THE DELEGATIONS
TO THE FORUM FOR PEACE AND
RECONCILIATION

FIANNA FÁIL

THE NEW IRELAND FORUM REPORT analysed the nature of the Northern Ireland problem, and the principles underlying its resolution, in a way that remains valid and that commanded the consensus of all the constitutional Nationalist Parties at that time and since. It provided important source material for the Anglo-Irish Agreement and the Joint Declaration.

THE NATURE OF THE PROBLEM

The problem of Northern Ireland remains the unresolved issue in relations between Britain and Ireland. It is the remaining product of a centuries old policy by Britain (and previously England) to control Ireland for its own strategic reasons, a policy that has now been disclaimed in the Downing Street Declaration. In the process, two political traditions were forged, one whose primary loyalty was to Britain, and the other whose focus of loyalty was on Ireland and its people.

One of the enduring legacies of that policy, even when the need for it has long since disappeared, is the persistence of a deeply divided community in Northern Ireland. Over the past two centuries great efforts have been made to unite the two traditions, for example by the

United Irishmen, Young Ireland, and the cultural revival, but they did not have lasting success in overcoming the deeper divisions. Initiatives of unionist origin to the same end included the Wyndham land purchase scheme, the Co-operative Movement, the Irish Association of 1938, and the reformist tendency of Captain O'Neill and the power-sharing experiment led by Brian Faulkner. In other movements, the divisions between the two traditions were exploited and widened for political reasons to try and prevent Home Rule for Ireland and, failing that, to win the exclusion of Ulster, with paramilitary means being used to exercise a unionist veto. This accelerated a resort to force on the nationalist side to win full independence for Ireland and, in turn, the price for this involved a forced acceptance of partition as a *fait accompli* in 1921. The successful opposition to Sunningdale later followed the same pattern as 1914. In contrast, the Anglo-Irish Agreement was maintained by the British Government despite massive unionist street protests.

The 1920-1 settlement broadly satisfied the desire for independence of the majority in the South, and the unionist desire to remain under continuing separate British jurisdiction. The guarantees on paper in the Government of Ireland Act, 1920, of non-discrimination, proportional representation, and North-South institutions intended to lead to eventual reunification (and of a Boundary Commission), were all quickly scrapped or ignored. Both the formation of the State of Northern Ireland in line with the wishes of the unionist tradition, and its practice as a one-Party hegemony that actively discriminated against the minority, meant that it failed to win nationalist consent.

The demands for equality and civil rights in the late 1960s were not accommodated by the Unionist Government, and were strenuously resisted by elements within the unionist population. Attempts at repression and ensuing violence contributed to the collapse of internal political institutions in Northern Ireland in 1972. No effort to restore them since has been successful for any length of time. In their absence, the British Government has assumed direct political responsibility for Northern Ireland. The violence of the last twenty five years has undoubtedly contributed to and reinforced the prolonged political stalemate.

The problem can be expressed as an absence of political consensus at the most fundamental level. While unionists withhold their consent from a united Ireland, Northern nationalists have to a greater or lesser degree withheld their consent from Northern Ireland as a legitimate political entity.

The rest of the Irish people, in the South, whatever their continuing reservations about the original legitimacy of partition and certainly their rejection of its one-sided practice, have virtually all come to accept at this point that it would be wrong as well as impractical to coerce the people of Northern Ireland into a united Ireland, against the wishes of a majority there. This view is clearly expressed by the Taoiseach in the Downing Street Declaration.

PRINCIPLES UNDERLYING A RESOLUTION

Any new political agreement must have substantial cross-community support, and, since it must also deal with North-South relations, should constitute a new act of self-determination by the Irish people, exercised concurrently. The British Government have accepted in the Joint Declaration that the Irish people, North and South, will alone determine their future. The British Government must play an active role, as they have undertaken to do in the Joint Declaration, in promoting an agreement between them.

The resolution of the Northern Ireland problem over time and the establishment of a just and lasting peace will depend on agreement being reached on the following principles, among others:

A balanced accommodation needs to be further developed which will accommodate in the short- to medium-term fundamental and legitimate constitutional differences, and provide a framework whereby they can be democratically resolved both now and in the future. Such an accommodation must preserve the inalienable birthright to Irish citizenship of those living in the North.

The bedrock of any viable political consensus in the North must be establishment of full equality of treatment and parity of esteem for both the individuals and the communities from which they come, with democratic institutions in Northern Ireland based on the principle of partnership.

The setting up of democratically mandated North-South institutions with executive powers is essential, both for practical reasons to serve common interests between North and South against the backdrop of the European Single Market, and for reasons of identity as a reflection of the Irish dimension.

The negotiation of political settlement should be accompanied in parallel by, and culminate in, a comprehensive programme of demilitarisation, a fundamental reform of policing to make it more acceptable across the community, and the restoration of civil liberties.

Reconciliation and trust between both communities in Northern Ireland and both traditions in Ireland should be established by other confidence-building measures.

Efforts to reach an agreement based on these principles and putting them into practice are indispensable if we wish in time to be able to move on to the stage of Irish unity by agreement, which remains a valid long-term goal.

SOCIAL DEMOCRATIC
AND LABOUR PARTY

INTRODUCTION

IT SEEMS TRITE TO SAY THAT BEFORE we seek solutions to problems, we must analyse, define and agree on the nature of the problem. Time and time again the SDLP has discovered that the assumption of agreement on the nature of the problem is a totally false assumption. It is only on the basis of agreeing the extent and nature of the problem, and understanding and appreciating another's *perception* of it, that progress can be made. The SDLP has said this over and over again: analyse the problem and only *then* can the requirements to resolve it be realistically identified.

This process must be gone through before we can move anywhere near discussion about structures, institutions or re-organisation. Indeed, it can be said that the nature of the problem, and the perception of it, are in a state of change almost on a daily basis.

This Forum is an unique opportunity to maximise the process of problem analysis.

THE NATURE OF THE PROBLEM

ORIGIN

The origin of the Northern Ireland problem is intrinsically the relationship between the two islands of Ireland and Britain, and has been described as the 'last negative legacy of the ancient quarrel between the peoples of these islands'.

It must be clear that the ultimate resolution can only come about within the framework of the Anglo-Irish process. We must believe in our ability to establish a new basis of mutual trust leading to an irreversible healing process.

Some aspects of the problem are readily discernible, for instance, the question of identities. Indeed the *conflict* of the two identities in Northern Ireland is the essence of the problem, and the failure to provide structures of accommodation for both its continuance. Some will argue that there are several identities, but I address the simplest analysis which is that of *nationalist* and *unionist*.

NATIONALISTS

The nationalist community sees itself as essentially Irish and its home as the wider Irish family of the entire island of Ireland. Its vision and aspirations have moved considerably over the past two decades. Instead of defining itself in terms of anti-British separatism, it now conceives of itself more comprehensively as creating a new Ireland:

> ... a society within which, subject only to public order, all cultural, political and religious belief can be freely expressed and practised. Fundamental to such a society are freedom of conscience, social and communal harmony, reconciliation and the cherishing of the diversity of all traditions.

The nationalist identity was denied political expression and validity, and excluded from effective participation in the institutions of Government. Generally speaking, the nationalist vision was first acknowledged as a legitimate aspiration in the Sunningdale Agreement of 1973, expanded upon in the Anglo-Irish Agreement of 1985; its legitimacy was confirmed in the declaration of principles in the Downing Street Declaration of 1993, and incorporated in the Joint Framework Document of 1995.

For the nationalist community that 'Irish dimension' must be a fundamental element in any new arrangements that might emerge.

UNIONISTS

The unionist community, as we understand it, perceives itself as British with an underlying Protestantism which finds a strength in allegiance to the British Crown, relative to the latter's essential Protestantism. It sees the Irish nationalists' aspiration as a *threat* to its identity, and as being incapable of tolerance and respect for the unionist ethos, its heritage, tradition and civil liberties. Yet we must be conscious of the affinity felt by an increasing number of unionists with their Irishness, and who see themselves as Irish.

To protect this identity unionists felt a need to exercise total control and power exclusively. Whatever emerges from our debate – or other negotiations – it must embody a guarantee to accommodate the unionist ethos and way of life.

The last two decades of violence have greatly increased and emphasised these different identities, making our task much more difficult. The SDLP again wants to avail of this opportunity to repeat its denunciation of violence – being evil in itself – and also as a major force in perpetuating mistrust and division.

On this basis, then, certain *realities* present themselves.

PRINCIPLES UNDERLYING A RESOLUTION

POLITICAL PROCESS

A divided people can only be brought together in peace and justice by means of the *political process* towards an *agreed* future, which protects and promotes the interests of both communities and identities.

Three Relationships

We believe that such an agreed future can be addressed and resolved only in the context of three central relationships — within Northern

Ireland, within the island of Ireland and between Ireland and Britain. These relationships are totally interlocking and interdependent and have already been agreed to as such, by the two Governments and four of the Northern Parties.

The keys, therefore are:

(i)   accommodation of difference and

(ii) consent.

Sharing the island of Ireland

Failure to bring peace and stability to Ireland is the direct result of our inability to agree how to share this island, and how to evolve working relationships between the two communities – only political consensus can achieve this.

Anglo-Irish Agreement

The Anglo-Irish Agreement represents an irreversible breakthrough in understanding and tackling the underlying causes of Anglo-Irish conflict; a permanent mechanism for consultation and interaction, and an internationally recorded agreement with major implications for both communities with mutual assurances in Article 1 and a formal recognition of the Irish Government's right to be involved in the affairs of Northern Ireland.

CHANGES IN EUROPE AND BEYOND

Looking to Europe, changes in the relationship between the two countries which are occurring in the context of the European Union are of particular significance. We are all aware of the process in which the evolving Community will require the pooling of sovereignty by the Member States so as to meet common tasks. Clearly, these developments have the most profound implications for our relationships on this island.

HUMAN RIGHTS REALITIES

The problem we address has had the most profound implications for the whole issue of human rights, particularly in the legal, security and policing areas.

Law and order in democratic countries and, in particular, the introduction of emergency measures depend on a basic *consensus* about society itself and its institutions. Present security policies have arisen from the absence of political consensus. In Northern Ireland extraordinary security actions have taken place that call into question the effectiveness of the normal safeguards of the legal process.

Emergency legislation has been at the heart of the Northern Ireland legal structure since partition. Clearly, such a situation is ultimately unsustainable. Again, the lesson is clear: a basis for political consensus must be found.

PARAMILITARIES

The abuses of human rights on the part of the paramilitaries have been direct and horrific throughout the past twenty five years. Prior to the ceasefires, these paramilitary organisations set new lows in the despicable nature of their crimes. Their murders displayed a level of callousness and viciousness which indicates a comprehensive erosion of basic human values. It is also clear that a pervasive element of gangsterism has entered into the activities of many of the paramilitaries – protection rackets, drugs etc. The ceasefires have not eradicated such activities.

SECURITY FORCES

The security forces themselves *often* contribute to the problem. Too many people in Northern Ireland have experienced the reality of the power of the State, primarily through arbitrary, often gratuitously, intimidating and insulting searches of their person and property and the ultimate lawlessness of the shoot to kill policy. Yet, for many years, the British authorities have accepted that there can be no solution in security terms alone to the violence in Northern Ireland. It is then one of the bitter ironies of the Northern situation that the activities of the security forces have in fact at times contributed to the perpetuation of the violence they sought to prevent over the twenty five years of turmoil and trauma.

POLICING

The *policing issue* is of crucial and immediate importance. Impartial policing which commands support and confidence is essential to the well-being of any society. Fundamental changes in policing will be crucial in any new wider arrangements which may emerge from the current process.

The SDLP has put forward proposals on civil and security policing which hopefully will be the subject of further debates.

THE ECONOMIC AND SOCIAL REALITIES

ECONOMIC COSTS: DIRECT AND INDIRECT

The cost to the economies of both the United Kingdom and the Republic of Ireland has been measured in tens of billions of pounds – scarce resources which could have developed the economies of the island of Ireland.

Unemployment in Northern Ireland is over twice the overall British rate. Manufacturing productivity has dropped; and many of the traditional industries crucial to the Northern Ireland economy have become obsolete.

The *tourism industry,* has been severely hampered as a direct consequence of the continuing violence and instability. Elsewhere, tourism has been the major growth industry of the past two decades, but not in Ireland – North and South.

Indirect costs must take account of the fact that Northern Ireland has not fared as well in its dealings with the European Union as it might have done. This is largely the consequence of its being represented by a Government whose priorities in many respects differ radically from the needs of the people and economy of Northern Ireland.

HUMAN COSTS OF VIOLENCE

No one can calculate the cost in human misery inflicted on the victims of violence and their families over the past twenty five years. No less victims are those in both communities who have been caught up in all forms of violence, their lives and the lives of their families blighted by imprisonment and injustice. A deep and ongoing problem in this area must receive our urgent attention.

HUMAN COSTS — DEPRIVATION AND MARGINALISATION

One of the tragic legacies of a system of government which, for over fifty years, effectively denied one community an equality of social and economic opportunity has been the creation of severely marginalised and disadvantaged areas mainly within the nationalist community. The deprivation is, however, not confined to the nationalist community alone. As a result of the contraction of Northern Ireland's traditional industrial base, a new generation of workers from the unionist community has been reduced to a similar status of socio-economic marginalisation.

It is scarcely surprising — although no less of a tragedy for that — that it is from these areas that the paramilitaries draw some of their strongest support, with the sense of economic exclusion both contributing to, and exacerbating, the violence and instability. Moreover, the vicious circle of cause and effect has become so mutually reinforcing that it is very difficult to disentangle the tentacles of political *alienation* from those of *economic and social marginalisation*.

CONCLUSION

The foregoing is by no means an exhaustive outline of the nature of the Northern Ireland problem; it serves, however, to identify the main elements as the SDLP sees them. We look forward to a dialogue with the other Parties on our analysis and to a full exchange on how they perceive the situation. As we said at the beginning, such an exchange is essential if we are to move constructively, and with some prospect of success, to the even more difficult challenge of devising an equitable and enduring settlement.

FINE GAEL

THE NATURE OF THE PROBLEM

THE OBJECTIVE OF ANALYSING THE NATURE of the problem is a critically important task for this Forum. Fine Gael believe that fundamental to the problem we face are the different allegiances of different groups in Ireland. Some view their allegiance primarily in a British context, others see their allegiance in an Irish context, while still others have a primary allegiance to 'Ulster'. The task of this Forum is realistically to accommodate difference with acceptable political institutions which will gain the allegiance and the respect of all groups. In this regard we completely accept the right of each group to aspire to its fundamental goal and indeed its right to attempt to persuade others through peaceful means to achieve that goal. However, in making accommodation a reality we must be prepared to visualise a new context for the problem. The task is to create an inclusive solution which will gain the allegiance of all.

As stated, Fine Gael believe that central to the nature of the problem we face are fundamental differences between various groups who live on the island and who have different political allegiances. Principal to this are the major traditions of Irish unionism and Irish nationalism. The key objective at this point in time must be to reconcile the two prominent traditions that exist on the island. That task is a difficult one, as the fundamental aspiration of each tradition is in conflict with the other. While recognising the prominence of Irish nationalism and Irish unionism, politicians should also begin to realise the importance of other groups. Modern Ireland has many political standpoints. Within the island, some citizens of both jurisdictions view themselves outside either traditional nationalism or unionism. The objective of European integration has created for many a new focus of political allegiance and has also helped to change the view of Ireland in the wider European and global context.

While the aspirations of nationalism or unionism are built on the fundamental question of the existence of partition, many within both communities would now prefer new arrangements involving power - or responsibility-sharing, joint authority or new North-South bodies. We must recognise the reality of the present situation, that a majority of people in Northern Ireland wish to remain within the United Kingdom. Those who would wish to persuade Unionists that they should enter into different constitutional arrangements with the rest of the island must face the fact that a solution will have to include a real accommodation of their Britishness. We believe that national allegiance takes many forms and that portraying the problem exclusively on a nationalist/unionist model fails to explain its true nature.

In attempting to understand fundamental differences of allegiance it is important to explain the complex nature of the problem. Simple territorial solutions will not work, as both Irish unity and the present status quo fail to take full consideration of the other allegiances. Therefore, any solution to the problem requires imagination in order to build an acceptable constitutional and institutional model which will gain the allegiance of all. This will require the agreement of all groups. Simple majoritarian rule will not solve the problem we face, as it is by definition complex and multifaceted.

Because of their differences of allegiance, it is important to assess the identities of all groups and the respect given to their symbols and traditions. Because of the rich and varied nature of Irish-British culture, it is important that the outward expressions of group identity be recognised in law. In both parts of Ireland, different groups are in a majority position. Consequently, the groups' identities need expression in the wider society. However, we should be mindful of the need to display the widest possible range of identities that exist in the jurisdiction and to give effect to that in law. In accommodating diversity, the principal feature of a modern, agreed Ireland should be that of pluralism. Each State on the island must begin to realise that within it there exist many groups who have different values, cultures and traditions. It is the job of the State to ensure that all groups feel equally at home, whatever political setting they live in. Therefore, simple delineation of nationality and creed needs to be detached from the fundamental law of the State and the exercise of power.

Because of the past twenty five years of violence and the negative images that have come from that, many people in the Republic and in Britain have lost interest in the problem. This helps to fuel alienation amongst both Northern nationalists and unionists, encouraging a sense that they are being rejected by people with whom they have important symbolic and political links. There is a popular perception that people in Britain 'don't care' while people in the Republic are 'switched off'. Both communities suffer alienation while their perceived compatriots in other parts of Britain and Ireland have seemed to move ahead of the political situation and are focussing on new political arrangements.

PRINCIPLES UNDERLYING A RESOLUTION

ANGLO-IRISH PROCESS

The Anglo-Irish process is central to any resolution of the problem. In this, Fine Gael believe that both the Anglo-Irish Agreement and the Downing Street Declaration provide an important foundation for any new agreement reached between both Governments and all the Parties in Northern Ireland. Fundamental to the Anglo-Irish process is the dynamic that all groups who have different political allegiances on the island are to be included in a future political settlement.

NON-VIOLENCE

Any resolution of the problem can only be achieved through democratic, non-violent, political action. In this regard, violence or the implicit threat of violence, can have no place in the modern Ireland. While Fine Gael welcome the Republican and Loyalist ceasefires, large amounts of explosives and weapons exist and must now be decommissioned.

PARITY OF ESTEEM

Before a resolution can be reached, it is important to state that a proper recognition of the identity of all groups in Ireland must now be put in place. This will require changes in Northern Ireland, particularly in regard to the Irish language, Irish flag and other symbols of the minority tradition. There is also a need to establish a greater trust in the present policing arrangements. We believe it obvious that without necessary changes to the policing of Northern Ireland, which are required to make it acceptable to all sections of the community, a lasting solution will not be possible. Concurrent change in the Republic should also be put in place in regard to the validity of the unionist/British tradition in Ireland. Irish nationalists must begin fully to understand the importance of the Britishness of unionist people in Northern Ireland. Parity of esteem is a two-way process involving compromise and understanding from all groups. In all matters we believe that a true equality of the traditions' outward expressions should exist before any resolution be reached.

MAKING POSITIVE GAINS

In our opening statement Fine Gael emphasised the view that politicians often present the Northern Ireland problem as a zero sum game, where for one to gain the other must lose. A resolution of the problem requires making positive gains for all groups who are involved. This task is difficult, but is surely a central principle behind the resolution of the problem. We believe that change is required both in the Government of Ireland Act and in Articles 2 and 3 of the 1937 Constitution. Such constitutional change could help to transform the situation and make positive gains for both communities. Equally, a Bill of Rights for Northern Ireland, setting out specific rights for all citizens, could be seen as a gain for all communities.

BUILDING COMMON GROUND

The principle of building common ground between all parties is of paramount importance. Agreements reached on a local level between cross-community groups should be seen as a priority. A resolution of the problem can only come about with a step-by-step approach.

The sharing of power in some local authorities in Northern Ireland has helped to build trust and confidence between local communities.

In building common ground we should also be mindful of the role of education in that process. Strengthening the role of integrated education and developing more extensive programmes of education in mutual understanding are also important.

THE LABOUR PARTY

INTRODUCTION

IN THIS FORUM WE SEEK TO CONFRONT the legacy of history and the facts of geography. The realities they dictate to us undermine many of our cherished dreams and most wishful thinking. Northern Ireland is not Yorkshire or Essex, serenely and unquestionably British in its character and destiny. Unionists are not lapsed members of the United Irishmen, waiting to snap out of a temporary aberration.

These facts must be acknowledged. We cannot change the reality that there are two traditions on this island, each strongly determined to maintain its distinctive ethos and identity and each deeply fearful of being the ultimate loser. We have a choice only about how we respond to these realities.

LABOUR – PART OF A THIRD STRAND

In common with most of the other democratic socialist/social democratic parties, Labour define their priorities in terms of the well-being and empowerment of individuals and communities. The focus of our policies is and always has been the living standards of people and the communities in which we live. For many years the Party was strongest amongst organised labour and our priorities were dictated by that fact.

In recent decades the Party have broadened their agenda – and their support base – by reflecting the demands of people in the areas of health, education and housing. We have sought to promote a pluralist and more inclusive society, and have sought to campaign for an open and accountable relationship between the political system and the people it serves.

The Labour Party was founded before partition. One of the founders of our Party, James Larkin, spent much time developing the trade union movement amongst the working class people of Belfast, many of them Protestant. James Connolly, himself a Scot, was hardly a traditional nationalist. His words are as relevant today as they were when they were written:

> Ireland without her people is nothing to me, and the man that is bubbling over with enthusiasm for 'Ireland' and can yet pass unmoved through our streets and witness all the wrong and suffering, the shame and degradation wrought on the people of Ireland, aye, wrought by Irishmen upon Irishmen and Irishwomen, without burning to end it is, in my opinion, a fraud and a liar in his heart, no matter how he loves that combination of chemical elements that he is pleased to call Ireland.

For many years the Labour Party saw themselves as straddling and transcending the traditions of unionism and nationalism. We set out to improve the standard of living for all our people and to give as many people as possible a say in the institutions which decide their lifestyles and those of their children. Our philosophy is by definition an internationalist one. Many in our Party and many of our supporters are not comfortable with traditional nationalism and unionism, particularly in their most jingoistic manifestation. There are many who would argue that national identity should be secondary to questions of social and economic interest and self-interest. In this we are but one part of a third strand in Irish society, a section of our people which does not see itself as *exclusively* informed by the ethos of either of the two primary traditions.

There are many such people in Ireland both North and South. There are numerous voluntary and community groups which seek to straddle the community divide. The *Opsahl Report* points out that women's groups and groups dominated by women have been particularly successful in this regard. The trade union movement and many sporting organisations and professional bodies have also succeeded to a greater and lesser extent. The role and success of such groups in accommodating difference is something on which we can build.

That said, it is clearly wishful thinking to believe that matters of national identity and allegiance can be set aside or wished away. The continuing conflict of national allegiances has stunted the growth of 'normal' Party politics in the South and virtually prevented it in the North. Working class Protestants in Northern Ireland vote for one Party whilst working class Catholics vote for another. Both are victims of political discrimination and social injustice. But the Party political system does not provide a means by which this inequality can be addressed. In part, this is a result of the lack of political leadership but it would be facile to suggest that this is the only reason.

For most (but not all) people in Northern Ireland, the question of national identity and allegiance is primary. There will never be normal left/right politics until the greater constitutional question is dealt with in a manner which satisfies the greatest possible number of people. For the moment we are driven to the inescapable conclusion that there are two traditions in Northern Ireland, two traditions which make up a deeply divided society.

THE NATURE OF THE PROBLEM

ACCOMMODATION OF RIGHTS

The problem of Northern Ireland is one of two sets of rights. The position of each tradition is logical and justifiable in its own eyes. The dilemma is that, at the *extremes* and as traditionally stated, the two sets of rights are incompatible.

This incompatibility of the extremes has brought about twenty five years and more of bloody conflict. Thousands have died because of the violent rejection by one tradition of the rights and realities of the other.

The alternative path is to accept these realities. We can build new political arrangements on the reciprocal acceptance of our differences and on the rules we devise to manage them. We must work for peaceful reconciliation of differences and agreement on structures which will safeguard the interests of both traditions.

TWO TRADITIONS – MANY FACETS

Neither tradition in Ireland is homogeneous. Many unionists see themselves as both Irish and British and see no contradiction. It often surprises observers to find that many unionists are instinctively anti-English. They do not identify closely with the people of Essex or Kent. This in no way takes from their own sense of themselves as British. They owe allegiance to Britain whilst still proudly thinking of themselves as Irish. Many Scottish and Welsh people would hold a similar view of themselves.

Nevertheless, there are unionists who disdain and dislike the description of themselves as Irish. They believe themselves to be as British as Finchley and would like to be seen and treated as such.

It is clear that many people in the rest of the United Kingdom do not see Northern Ireland as British in any meaningful way. This is profoundly upsetting for many unionists and there are now many who would be prepared to 'go it alone' if circumstances demanded it. Self-reliance and self-esteem are two proud features of the unionist community.

All strands of unionism share two things: they see themselves as British and they feel threatened by the Republic and by nationalists within Northern Ireland.

The nationalist or Catholic community is equally diverse in its make-up and expression. Many Catholics feel a deep sense of grievance. They suffered decades of discrimination and oppression. This discrimination was both political and socio-economic. There are doubtless some Catholics who would be happy with the present constitutional arrangement if economic discrimination were redressed and internal structures of government were put in place in Northern Ireland which would guarantee their rights.

Some Catholics are scarcely nationalist at all. Approximately one quarter of Catholics do not vote for Nationalist Parties. Many of these are middle class, and some work in institutions which actively sustain

British jurisdiction (e.g. the law, the civil service etc.). That is not to say that all Catholic public servants actively support partition. This is not so. What is clear is that many of them do not see the end of partition as a priority.

Nevertheless, a substantial majority of Catholics continue to support Nationalist Parties whose aim is the ending of partition. Even amongst them there are substantial differences. Some nationalists are prepared to accept interim arrangements provided their national identity and tradition are given adequate expression in their governing institutions. Others will settle for nothing less than an end to partition, British withdrawal and a unitary state.

The diversity within both traditions is a critical factor which must be addressed when seeking ways of accommodating our differences. It is simply not possible to bring about full integration with Britain and a unitary Irish state at the same time. But there is much in between which can be reconciled and there are many in both communities who are willing and anxious to bring about that reconciliation.

THE WIDER CONTEXT — BRITAIN AND IRELAND

It is not only in Northern Ireland that attitudes have changed in recent years. In the Republic and Britain too things are no longer as they used to be.

Successive opinion surveys over many years have shown that many people in the Republic attach little significance to Northern Ireland in determining their attitude to politics. Support for a united Ireland is still strong but there are a substantial minority who are actively opposed to it or simply don't care. A recent survey suggested that only a small section of people in the Republic would be prepared to pay more taxes in order to bring about a united Ireland. The response to this question can hardly be considered definitive in that the question was hypothetical in the extreme. Nonetheless, the nature of the response must give cause for thought to those who automatically assume that everybody in the Republic would support an end to partition in whatever circumstances that came about.

The great majority of people in the Republic identify in the first instance with Northern nationalists. A majority in the Republic aspire to a united Ireland but it would be foolish to ignore the fact that this aspiration is weaker and less widespread than it was twenty five years ago. The reasons for this change are relatively clear. It is now seventy years since partition and many people, most particularly young and urban people, now regard it as a fact of life. Greater economic prosperity and the development of a more cosmopolitan lifestyle have also played a role. So too has Ireland's membership of the European Union.

The existence of violent conflict in the North has led many in the South to question the old certainties and values. The aspiration of many in the South to a united Ireland has been greatly weakened by the very fact that some people in the North have been prepared to engage in an armed struggle in order to bring it about.

Until 1968 Northern Ireland scarcely figured on the British agenda. The British people as a whole paid little attention to Northern Ireland, while Westminster Governments acquiesced in the creation of a sectarian state within the United Kingdom. The Civil Rights movement in the 1960s and 70s and the armed struggle of the IRA have changed all that. In recent years the increased level of 'Loyalist violence' has also affected British opinion.

Few people in the rest of the United Kingdom feel any great affinity with Northern Ireland. While the political establishment is committed to continuing the current position, a substantial minority of people would happily withdraw from Northern Ireland if they thought this could be done without risk of serious civil disorder or worse. The majority of people are prepared to continue the huge level of financial subsidy whilst the Westminster Government seeks to bring about a solution to the problem.

Indeed, it can be argued that the British Government was doing no more than catching up on public opinion throughout its jurisdiction when it declared in the Joint Declaration and elsewhere that it had no selfish or strategic interest in Northern Ireland. The expression of that sentiment as a definitive statement of policy is nonetheless welcome for that.

For many years it could reasonably have been assumed that the views of nationalists in the North were similar to, or compatible with, those of most people in the Republic. It would also have been assumed that Northern unionists could depend on the support of the Westminster establishment. It can no longer be assumed that this will always be the case.

VIOLENCE

Labour have always rejected the use of violence as a means of political expression. The use of violence has retarded the reconciliation of differences which is essential to any political agreement between the peoples of this island. We warmly welcome the recent repudiation of violence by both Republican and Loyalist paramilitary organisations. We salute the courage and foresight of those who helped bring this about.

PRINCIPLES UNDERLYING RESOLUTION

POLITICAL AGREEMENT

Labour accept the three-stranded approach of negotiations used hitherto. We also accept the principle that nothing can be agreed until everything is agreed. Any future agreement will include:

1. Internal Structures: While no lasting accommodation can be based on exclusively internal arrangements within Northern Ireland, democratic and evolved methods of government for the Province will be an essential component of any settlement. It is generally accepted that there can be no monopoly of power under any new internal institutions in Northern Ireland, and no return to the majoritarian, and often authoritarian structures of old. Any devolved government must draw from and adequately represent both traditions and must be capable of attracting the widespread support of both traditions.

2. The two Governments and any assembly which may be set up in Northern Ireland must accept the equal legitimacy of the two allegiances and the right of those who profess them to equal respect. The principle of equality of esteem and parity of treatment must inform all the activities of government in Northern Ireland.

3. Labour support the establishment of democratically mandated cross-border bodies with executive powers. Once established, these

bodies must be accountable in a fashion to be agreed by negotiations. Such bodies are needed for practical, political, and symbolic reasons.

It is manifestly in the interests of both parts of Ireland that policies in relation to a wide range of matters should be coordinated. In some cases coordination will involve harmonising the legislative, regulatory and administrative framework within which policy operates. Areas like industrial development, the attraction of inward investment, trade and tourism promotion, transport, energy and communications, and many aspects of social policy, in addition to a wide range of cultural and sporting activities lend themselves to the development of a much more coordinated approach towards their implementation.

The implementation of agreed, island-wide policies will inevitably require the executive functioning of the bodies carrying them out. An all-island approach is also essential if we are to maximise the benefits of our common EU membership and interests.

4.   Labour support a fundamental reform of policing in Northern Ireland. We also believe that measures should be taken to deal with the exceptional quantities of arms and explosives in the hands of paramilitaries. The question of legally held arms must also be addressed. British troops should be withdrawn from the streets of Northern Ireland as soon as this can be safely done.

5.   Labour support the introduction of a Bill of Rights – probably based on the European Convention. We would be well disposed to amending the Republic's Constitution so as to include similar rights and means of redress in the Republic's basic law where these do not already exist.

6.   Labour support the creation of a pluralist society in the Republic and in Northern Ireland. Whilst recognising the excellent contribution made by the churches to our society, we nonetheless believe in the separation of church and State as a fundamental democratic principle. Matters of private morality should not be

dictated by law and it would be wholly wrong if the laws and practices in either part of Ireland were to disproportionately represent the views of one religion.

7. The principle of democratic control, accountability and participation must be widely extended throughout society not least in the sphere of education. The education systems North and South must be used to infuse a spirit of mutual understanding. Integrated education must be facilitated and provided where this is what parents want.

CONSTITUTIONAL CHANGE

Labour subscribe to the principle of consent set out in the Anglo-Irish Agreement and the Downing Street Declaration. We also support the concept of a balanced constitutional change.

We have never argued that Articles 2 and 3 should remain as if cast in bronze, incapable of change. Rather, we have argued that they should be seen as what they are − or rather what they were intended to be − part, and only part, of the constitutional description of our nation.

However, the Constitution was never intended to be an obstacle to mutual understanding on this island and our people would never wish it to be so. If in a new situation there is need − and we expect there will be − of a changed approach to reflect and buttress a new level of mutual understanding, we believe the Irish people will readily be persuaded to endorse change, provided that they are satisfied that it does truly serve that purpose.

We have all learned the hard way in Ireland that the territorial approach has served our relationship poorly. We know from experience that the policies of domination and denial, and the concepts of victory and defeat will never form the basis for understanding and peace between us.

It is not only possible, but even likely, that we will wish to explore other ways of defining our nation, for example, in terms of the people and communities which are its true essence.

In short, any settlement in relation to Northern Ireland will, and must, give rise to a *new* dispensation − new arrangements, new relationships, and a new constitutional underpinning. We believe that that new dispensation must be reflected in British and in Irish constitutional law.

Insofar as our own Constitution is concerned, we favour the substantial amendment of Articles 2 and 3, aimed primarily at removing the sense of territorial threat that inspires fear and anxiety in many parts of the Northern Ireland community. Our nation — the Irish nation — must be defined much more in terms of its people, in all the diversity of their identities and traditions, and much less in terms of territory. The territory of this island is a shared inheritance, and we must be prepared to recognise that. The principle of consent means that we must also be prepared to accept that there can be no change in the status of Northern Ireland without the consent of its people, and that we seek no right to exercise jurisdiction over Northern Ireland contrary to the will of its people.

CONCLUSION

This is a time of unprecedented hope and peace but there is much which is still to be done. We must all of us play our part in ensuring that the opportunity is not missed.

SINN FÉIN

THE NATURE OF THE PROBLEM

THE HISTORICAL DIMENSION

No British government ought ever to forget that this perilous moment, like many before it, is the outworking of a history for which our country is primarily responsible... Our injustice created the situation; and by constantly repeating that we will maintain it so long as the majority wish it, we actively inhibit Protestant and Catholic from working out a new future together. This is the root of violence...

DR JOHN AUSTIN BAKER, ANGLICAN BISHOP OF SALISBURY

BRITISH INTERFERENCE LIES AT THE ROOT of the political conflict on this island. We have a myriad of political, social and economic structures which sustain and encourage division, perpetuate the destructive politics of 'them and us' and feed the conflict that tears us further apart.

All of us share a degree of culpability for the unresolved conflict on this island and we share a responsibility to find the formula that will move us from that situation of conflict towards reconciliation, from a climate of disunity towards unity. But it is Sinn Féin's contention that the primary responsibility in all of this rests with Britain. It is because of British policy that our conflict exists and only a change in British policy can create the atmosphere necessary to resolve it.

The conflict which we have inherited is not an accident of history, but is the legacy of a deliberate strategy adopted by Britain towards its nearest neighbour. Fearing the implications of Irish independence, successive London governments adopted the classic colonial tactic of 'divide and rule', undermining effective opposition by encouraging internal discord.

Even the British Government would acknowledge that, whatever about the present situation, British policy on Ireland was driven in the past by strategic, military, economic and political imperatives. Partition is the product of that policy.

Currently, the British Government have amended their position by disclaiming any military or economic interest. However, they have refused to declare that they have no 'political' interest.

Peace in Ireland cannot be denied because of selfish political concerns in Westminster. The British Government should instead become persuaders for agreement on political structures in Ireland.

DIVISION, INEQUITY AND INJUSTICE

We declare that we desire our country to be ruled in accordance with the principles of Liberty, Equality and Justice for all.

DEMOCRATIC PROGRAMME OF THE FIRST DÁIL

Ours is a divided society. In common with other peoples, we are divided politically, economically and socially, rich from poor, men from women, young from old. There is a regional divide also, with wealth and power concentrated in a narrow geographic corridor outside of which the crisis of powerlessness has encouraged a haemorrhaging of young people and the decline of rural communities. In our cities, tremendous wealth sits uneasily alongside dire poverty, and powerlessness has generated a sense of alienation and despair in many areas.

Inequity and injustice occur, therefore, on many levels and it is our view that this Forum should, in the course of its deliberations, address the wider implications of inequality and the fundamental need for democratic control throughout Irish society.

As representatives of a section of the nation which has suffered collectively, which has experienced marginalisation, discrimination and oppression, we are conscious of the absolute requirement for laws and political structures which will command the respect of all sections of our people. Our vision is the transformation of Irish society, the creation of a democracy built on agreement not conflict, unity not division.

THE ISSUE OF VIOLENCE

Political conflict has periodically resulted in armed hostilities. Sinn Féin recognises that the existence of injustice, allied to the absence of any real prospect of redress, made political violence inevitable. We acknowledge the selfless contribution which successive generations of Irish men and women have given to their country by taking up arms in the pursuit of liberty.

We are mindful also of the human cost of violent conflict and its potential further to exacerbate division. Families are left to mourn the loss of loved ones through death or imprisonment. Communities endure the persistent pressure of life in a war-zone, their lives disrupted by draconian laws which make little distinction between combatant and non-combatant, ever-conscious of the possibility of violent death. It is a dreadful and abnormal situation and we are all victims. Our determination is that never again will Irish men and women feel the necessity to confront oppression through recourse to arms.

The historic IRA cessation of 31 August, and the Loyalist ceasefire of 13 October 1994, while providing a welcome boost to the process of finding an enduring settlement, are not of themselves peace. A process that does not seek to resolve the deep political divisions that afflict our people and our country is doomed to ultimate failure. We are convinced that a lasting peace can only be built on principles of justice, democracy and Irish self-determination.

A DIVIDED SOCIETY

As individuals and as a significant national minority, unionists have democratic rights which not only can be upheld but must be upheld in an independent Ireland. That is the democratic norm. That is an essential ingredient of peace and stability.

SINN FÉIN POLICY DOCUMENT, *Towards a Lasting Peace in Ireland*

Political division, with its attendant 'traditions', is evidence of a ruptured nation, not of two mutually exclusive peoples. In seeking to heal this rupture, our objective must be to identify and develop what we hold in common and to transcend what divides us.

Unionists will ask why they should abandon their political heritage. After all, the union has had benefits. It bestowed a privileged status on a national minority. It gave that minority a disproportionate degree of social, economic and political power. And when it seemed that national self-determination could no longer be resisted, it gave unionists, through partition, their own state. All of this has convinced them that they have more in common with the people of Britain than they have with the rest of the people of Ireland. Attachment to the Crown has strengthened that sense of difference and, by virtue of the Crown's explicit sectarian basis, has deepened division.

Against that, dependence on Britain has ensured that unionists live in fear of sell-out. Always uncertain, expecting betrayal at every turn, unionism sees enemies everywhere. Far from being able to determine their own political destiny, unionists realise that their future rests in the hands of a Government which, despite its rhetoric, does not have their interest at heart. They suspect that when it suits, Britain will leave Ireland, the union will end and they won't be able to stop it happening.

Apart from its relationship with Britain, unionism has had a troubled relationship with nationalist Ireland. Sinn Féin recognises that unionists fear domination and the loss of identity in a new Ireland. In terms of their attitudes, divisive and sometimes supremacist traditions have created a culture that views the rest of the people of Ireland with suspicion, hostility and even contempt. Separate development – a sure consequence of a political entity founded on sectarianism – in terms of where we live, where we socialise and where our children go to school, has reinforced this notion of difference.

Nationalists cannot reassure unionists that their constitutional position is secure, because we do not determine British policy either. Nor should we pretend that our objective is anything less than unity and national self-determination, because that would be a lie and unionists are not fools. Tampering with Articles 2 and 3, failing to articulate our political aspirations – lest they offend – neither course will provide adequate reassurance. Instead, their only consequence would be to reimpose the sense of isolation which northern nationalists have felt since partition.

What nationalists can do, however, is to assure unionists that we have no wish to coerce them into anything and we have no wish to dominate them. As victims of coercion and domination, we know that these inspire hostility rather than agreement, conflict rather than stability, division rather than unity. A just settlement cannot be built without their input and we invite them to join with the rest of the people of Ireland in formulating an agreed future.

THE FAILURE OF PARTITION

The failure of partition is the strongest argument for its abandonment
GERRY ADAMS, SINN FÉIN PRESIDENT

The border partitioning Ireland was contrived by a British government so as to ensure an artificially constructed unionist majority. The partitioned area had no basis in geography or history, and its proposal had the distinction of being opposed by both nationalists and unionists at the time.

The foremost consequence of partition was that it institutionalised sectarianism. Those differences in outlook, religion and tradition which provide the diversity that makes a healthy society, became instead lines of conflict. With its own judiciary, police force and parliament, unionism – confident of British support – set about the creation of a 'Protestant State for a Protestant people'.

Partition affects every aspect of Irish society. In the North it has created a failed political entity marred by economic apartheid, political repression and religious intolerance. In the South the political division resulting from partition has stunted normal political, economic and social development. Both States are in a deep and permanent crisis.

Whilst no-one would argue that there is a complete similarity between the political conditions in Ireland and in South Africa, it is obvious that lessons can be drawn.

For example, the proposal for a 'Whites' homeland was rejected in South Africa precisely because of a commonly accepted view that partition in Ireland had been a political and economic disaster. Even the White South African political Parties accepted that an inclusive democratic settlement would not be achieved within such an arrangement.

The unionist veto is a negative power, a power only to say 'no'. It is a major barrier to the consideration of democratic options that would include all the people of Ireland within an agreed framework. The unionist veto is no more than a British Government device. Sinn Féin firmly believes that so long as the unionists in the Six Counties are assured a veto over change, then there is neither reason nor incentive for them to move towards an accommodation with the rest of the Irish people. In our view the guarantee of a veto to unionists has inhibited political movement in Ireland for over seventy years. It is clearly a failed policy and has perpetuated the cycle of repression and resistance. What is required is a new and imaginative approach which tilts the balance away from the prohibitive and negative power of veto towards the positive power of consent, of considering consent, of negotiating consent.

PRINCIPLES UNDERLYING A RESOLUTION

TOWARDS A LASTING SETTLEMENT

A clear policy change by the British Government would create the dynamic in which, for the first time, the Irish people could reach a democratic accommodation and in which a process of national reconciliation and healing could begin. A lasting peace requires that unionist consent, agreement and allegiance to new political structures is gained. In the same way, the gaining of nationalist consent, agreement and allegiance to new political structures is required if we are to have a lasting peace. This clearly requires an end to all vetos, to all preconditions and to any attempt to impose a predetermined outcome to the exercise of national self-determination. Sinn Féin is willing to do all it can to advance the search for agreement and the building of trust in the context of the Forum for Peace and Reconciliation. Sinn Féin is convinced that the potential further to develop the peace process exists. The dynamic necessary to move us all out of conflict must be found in the principles, framework, timescale, procedures and objectives of a peace process and particularly in negotiation. The two Governments and the political Parties have a responsibility to ensure that this opportunity is not lost. We must all work to build progress and be prepared to demonstrate the courage and imagination necessary to advance the peace process.

THE
PROGRESSIVE DEMOCRATS

THE NATURE OF THE PROBLEM

WHEREAS THE ROOTS OF THE NORTHERN IRELAND problem lay in the Plantations of the sixteenth and seventeenth centuries, and the growth of Orangeism from the latter part of the eighteenth century, the key manifestation of the problem was the evolution of conflicting national allegiances on the island of Ireland during the nineteenth century.

As Irish nationalism evolved during the nineteenth century, it crystallised around the Irish Parliamentary Party's campaign for a separate, or Home Rule, Parliament for Ireland. As that campaign appeared to verge on victory with the passage of the Third Home Rule Bill in 1914 (its implementation being suspended because of the outbreak of the Great War), it accelerated a vigorous anti-Home Rule movement among Irish unionists, who were opposed to Irish nationalism; who saw the union link with Britain threatened, and, with it, their privileged position as the beneficiaries of the union.

With more violent and separatist nationalism eclipsing moderate Home Rule nationalism, through the 1916 Rising, and the routing of the Irish Parliamentary Party in the 1918 General Election, the crude compromise between separatist Irish nationalism and Britain on the one hand, and between Irish nationalism and Irish unionism, on the other, was the creation of the State of Northern Ireland and the Irish Free State, under the Government of Ireland Act 1920.

Whereas the partition arrangement under the 1920 Act was crude and anomalous in the extreme, and was intended to be revised by the Boundary Commission of 1924, the fact remains nonetheless that it was *a result,* rather than *the cause,* of division between Irish nationalists and unionists.

This point is of the most fundamental importance. Those who insist that partition is the root cause of the current problem are refusing to face up to the different and conflicting national allegiances on this island that pre-dated the partition settlement, precipitated its creation, and continue to underpin it.

Any notion that partition is primarily being maintained by the British Government is dispelled by the terms of the Downing Street Declaration, notably the British statement that 'they have no selfish strategic or economic interest in Northern Ireland', and that 'as a binding obligation', they will introduce legislation to give effect to a united Ireland, or 'to any measure of agreement on future relationships in Ireland which the people living in Ireland may themselves freely so determine' (para. 4).

With approximately twenty percent of the population of the island of Ireland committed to the maintenance of the union with Britain in the form of the Northern Ireland State, the basic problem quite simply is not one of the British presence, nor would it be solved by a 'Brits-Out' solution.

This is the case because there are approximately one million people in Northern Ireland of a unionist disposition, and the most likely consequence of a sudden, unilateral departure of British administration from Northern Ireland would be large-scale civil strife, likely to impact on the entire island, and possibly resulting in the eventual establishment of a redrawn and more homogeneously unionist Northern Ireland, but at a terrible price.

If the unionist allegiance of up to one million people, and their commitment to the union with Britain, is seen as one of the key elements in the Northern Ireland problem, it must also be recognised that the inability of the Northern Ireland establishment for the past seventy four years to accommodate and reflect the different national allegiance of approximately half a million non-unionists is equally the other key element of the problem.

As the Northern State evolved from the early 1920s it became more and more a unionist State for a unionist people, notwithstanding the fact that a third of the population of that State did not share its *raison d'être* or its ethos.

One of the amazing features of Northern Ireland is that at no stage, up to the abolition of the Stormont Parliament in 1972, was any real effort made by the unionist establishment to win the allegiance or support of a third of its citizens. Indeed, the minority were treated as the enemy within, and deprived of their full civil rights.

This only began to be redressed with the birth of the Civil Rights Movement in the late 1960s, and was accelerated under the period of direct British rule since 1972.

Given the failure to accommodate Irish nationalism within Northern Ireland, it was only reasonable and inevitable that the nationalist minority there felt alienated from the State of Northern Ireland, continued to aspire to all-Ireland unity, and reposed little faith in the prospects of being accorded a fair deal, or political accommodation, within Northern Ireland.

In varying degrees, they placed the blame for their plight on the unionist community, on the British Government for underpinning and sustaining unionist supremacy, and on the Republic in the South for largely ignoring their situation.

While this undoubtedly reflects the accumulated legacy of relationships between unionists and nationalists within Northern Ireland, two other factors must be taken into account in describing the nature of the problem.

One of these is the role of the British Government since the introduction of direct rule in 1972. There is little doubt that gradually over that period, the British have engineered significant social, economic and legal reforms in Northern Ireland that have tackled some, but not all, of the injustices suffered by nationalists under unionist rule, and the State of Northern Ireland is now a fairer, more democratic and more balanced society in terms of civil rights, economic entitlement and fair opportunity, than it was.

The other factor that is important is the evolution of society in the Republic of Ireland. In most respects, the Republic is now a post-nationalist society. It is no longer obsessed by its relationship with

Britain and its full membership of the wider European Union for the past twenty two years has given the Republic a greater sense of self-confidence, a much higher degree of economic independence and an appreciation that it can play a meaningful role in international affairs, including peace-keeping. The South has moved away from the heavily confessional and inward-looking society that characterised it in its earlier decades. It has largely benefited from healthier foreign influences and outlooks.

In the Republic, therefore, the sense of Irish identity is no longer seriously expressed in terms of anti-British or anti-English sentiment, in contrast to the way many nationalists in the North express their sense of identity.

A topical symbol of our national self-confidence in the Republic, and our ability to relate to Britain in a totally positive way, is the story of the Irish soccer manager.

The vast majority of people in the Republic have no time at all for the more extreme form of Irish nationalism as espoused by Sinn Féin/IRA. Their battle-cry of 'Brits Out' and their version of Irish national self-determination turn off most people in the Republic, and that is reflected in the lack of electoral support for Sinn Féin.

Furthermore, the IRA campaign of violence has made very many people in the Republic uncomfortable with the term 'Republican'; and has even killed interest in the very notion of Irish unity for many.

PRINCIPLES UNDERLYING A RESOLUTION

COMMITMENT TO PEACEFUL MEANS BY ALL PARTIES

The foremost principle must be a commitment by all sides to resolve the problem by peaceful means only. The abandonment of violence by both sets of paramilitaries has made this possible. Full credit is due to those who helped bring about the cessation of violence, and the task of all democratic politicians now is to ensure that the outbreak of peace is not accompanied by a rebirth of intransigence. The people of the entire island would never countenance a recommencement of terrorist violence.

If that principle can be accepted as binding on all sides, then everything is possible.

NORTHERN IRELAND NOT POLITICALLY HOMOGENEOUS

The elementary lesson of Northern Irish history is that it is not a politically homogeneous society. Unionism and nationalism tend to see one another as mutually exclusive, and majority-rule or winner-take-all political models are doomed to fail. Northern Ireland is both Irish and British, and a key principle is that governmental models must reflect and accommodate these conflicting loyalties in an unique way. Northern Ireland is *sui generis* and foreign models and parallels are of limited value. Protestant and Catholic Irish people do co-exist happily and fruitfully in the South and abroad. Neither sees the other as in any way a threat. They can eventually do so in Northern Ireland too, when neither sees the other as a threat and when neither seeks to dominate the other.

ACCEPT CURRENT STATUS

Another key principle in the search for a solution must be an acknowledgement of the constitutional status quo. Reciting historical wrongs, and disputing the legitimacy of the State of Northern Ireland will get us nowhere. In that context, we welcome the assurance given by the Irish Government in the Downing Street Declaration that: 'it would be wrong to attempt to impose a united Ireland, in the absence of the freely given consent of a majority of the people of Northern Ireland'.

All Parties should accept that we must all seek to move forward from where we now find ourselves, not from where we might wish to be, notwithstanding the historic reality of the undemocratic foundations of Northern Ireland.

REAL EQUALITY FOR NATIONALISTS

The next principle of any political settlement must be the guarantee, *and tangible delivery of* real and substantial equality for nationalists with unionists within Northern Ireland.

While it is politically unhelpful to recriminate about history, the path to reconciliation between the two communities in Northern Ireland must include a clear acknowledgement and redress of the massive wrong done by discrimination against nationalists, especially in the Stormont era, coupled with guarantees that discrimination will be completely eliminated.

Respect for nationalism must be institutionalised within Northern Ireland. Moreover, if a change in the Republic's Constitution is demanded to remove the territorial claim, it follows that Nationalism must be legally, institutionally and economically legitimised within Northern Ireland.

New laws to validate nationalist sentiment and aspirations must be part of any lasting reconciliation and settlement. Bigotry, triumphalism and sectarianism have no place in a society that cherishes both traditions equally.

Unionists must accept that the Catholic/nationalist community will not become reconciled to Northern institutions unless these are re-modelled to reflect the existence of two different traditions.

WRITTEN CONSTITUTION FOR NORTHERN IRELAND

As the next principle underlying a resolution the Progressive Democrats propose the creation of constitutional guarantees for the citizens of the North.

Given that Northern Ireland already has its own courts and things like special voting arrangements in Euro-elections and local elections, there is no real obstacle to giving Northern Ireland a written constitution, incorporating a Bill of Rights, and with its own constitutional court to guarantee them.

It is possible to envisage such measures extending beyond just individual rights to communal rights and encompassing judicial control of administrative, and legislative, acts. Such a judicial arm of State would be immensely more attractive to a nationalist minority.

Indeed, if Northern Ireland, while part of the United Kingdom, were given a constitution, which not only created a Bill of individual rights, but also recognised the majoritarian principle set down in Article 1 of the Hillsborough Agreement, and in the Downing Street Declaration, and expressly acknowledged the legitimacy of both unionist and nationalist aspirations, there would be more hope that both communities would give their loyalty to shared institutions. Such a Constitution would have to be adopted in a plebiscite held in Northern Ireland.

DEVOLVED GOVERNMENT

Another principle underlying a resolution of the problem is devolved government for Northern Ireland.

Models for devolution are well known, and are feasible. They need not be elaborated here. Suffice it to say that the process of reconciliation, and the evolution of responsible representative politics, is likely to be encouraged by the creation in Northern Ireland of an assembly, with a representative power-sharing executive, exercising that power in a manner that prevents the political exclusion of either tradition. Twenty two years of government from abroad is enough.

ARTICLES 2 AND 3

While many may feel that the unionist preoccupation with Articles 2 and 3 is a mere device to avoid other political change, and that their elimination would not alter unionist attitudes or sentiment, the Progressive Democrats believe that the maintenance of a claim of right by the people of the Republic to enforce their Constitution, Parliament and Government on the people and territory of Northern Ireland is not consistent with a wholehearted, unequivocal acceptance of the majoritarian principle set out in Article 1 of the Anglo-Irish Agreement and in the terms of the Downing Street Declaration.

We do not accept that the nationalist viewpoint and ideal can be given Constitutional expression only by such a claim of right. As was shown in 1967, it is possible to recast Article 3 (even without changing Article 2) so as to espouse the principle of Irish unity by consent.

We believe that if a new political settlement gave rise to a restatement of the 'three relationships' within these islands, including the legitimacy of the aspiration of Irish unity, then the voters of the Republic would agree to a Constitutional clause ratifying those arrangements in substitution for the present wording of Articles 2 and 3.

NEW NORTH-SOUTH INSTITUTIONS

The emergence of an entirely new relationship between Northern Ireland and the Republic would be another key principle of any durable political solution.

If the 'majoritarian principle' governing the current constitutional status of Northern Ireland is accepted *de jure* by the Republic through changing Articles 2 and 3, the basis for rejecting close North-South links and institutions by unionists as the 'thin end of the nationalist wedge' falls away.

A new North-South relationship, with accompanying institutions and agencies, would be immensely more achievable if the 'constitutional status' issue was resolved. The benefits of such closer cooperation and such North-South bodies are so obvious, in both the economic and social spheres, to both parts of the island, that their continued absence is an avoidable tragedy and damages all Irish people.

THE ALLIANCE PARTY

THE NATURE OF THE PROBLEM

THE ALLIANCE PARTY WAS BORN, in the aftermath of the outbreak of the present 'troubles', out of a commitment to heal the divisions in Northern Ireland by bringing about a fair and just society. Though our thinking has been further developed in various documents since, the starting point for an understanding of the Alliance analysis may be found in the statement of fundamental principles upon which the Party was founded in April 1970.

These identify Alliance as a liberal Party, committed to pluralism, tolerance, participatory democracy, respect for human rights, non-doctrinaire economic policies, and the necessity of an impartial but firm application of the rule of law.

The principles also identify the constitutional dispute as being at the root of all our most fundamental difficulties in creating a pluralist Northern Ireland, and affirm that it is for the people of Northern Ireland to determine their own future.

It can be no surprise therefore that when the Joint Declaration was published by the British and Irish Governments on 15 December 1993, Alliance gave an immediate and fully supportive response. That declaration, in its rejection of violence as a legitimate political instrument, its affirmation of the imperative of respect for human rights, and its watershed commitment to the requirement for separate consent from the people of Ireland, North and South, is regarded by Alliance as an international expression of some of our most cherished views.

These principles suggest some of the elements which may form a constitutional settlement, and we have in other places, and at other times, outlined our preferred structural options. We may revisit these proposals later in the life of the Forum, but first we have been asked to outline our analysis of the nature of the problem.

We must start by noting the very ancient nature of our feud. It is no new thing for the North to be the scene of struggle. Centuries before the Reformation brought its religious divisions, and long before England was England, and began its struggle for control of the islands, the legendary Cuchulainn was defending Ulster against Queen Maeve. In more reliable history we are informed that when Congal of Ulster was fighting with Domhnal of Meath as far back as 637 AD his support came from his friends in Scotland. This suggests that there has never been a simple unity of the people of Ireland, that the Northern people have long had a sense of separateness, and often felt closer to those who lived across the Channel in Scotland, than they did to those in the South-West of the island. This is not strange, for we usually build up relationships with those we can meet easily and frequently, and the stretch of water between Antrim and Galloway has, throughout history, been as much a channel of communication as a boundary. For this and many other historical reasons, the people of the North, with their many different origins, religious views, political affiliations, and cultural attachments, have always been seen as forming a community, though without precise geographical boundaries.

Superimposed on the natural development of this and other communities, there has been the historic struggle for control of land in this archipelago of islands. The people of England, for many centuries sought to extend their control to include all the islands. This was expressed politically in the unionist, or British nationalist, view that all the people on these islands should form one nation state. It found its expression in the United Kingdom, though a full political integration, the aim of unionism, was never achieved. This British nationalist view, and particularly the attempts to enforce it, often in most unjust and cruel ways, provoked a natural reaction, the development of a strong Irish nationalism. This rebelled against British nationalism by expressing the view that it was not the people of these islands, but the people of Ireland, that should form a nation state. A whole mythology was created to support this view, and the real historic divisions of origin, religious affiliation, political conviction, and cultural diversity, were submerged in the struggle to create a separate Irish Republic, characterised by Gaelic culture, and Roman Catholic practice.

These struggles are not unique. The fight for control of land, even between siblings, is a common feature of life, no less in rural Ireland than elsewhere. It is also worth noting that those who devote themselves to striving for control of land or property often acquire them at the cost of good relationships. That excessive pressure from one group produces an equal and opposite reaction is a very familiar observation in human life, and not least in politics, and I am sure that you will have observed, if not indeed experienced, the fact that rivals can find themselves forced into taking up a particular position, simply in contrast to their opponent. Thirdly, the drive to create a nation state is a strong one. It is an attempt to include within certain borders as many of 'my people' as possible, while keeping 'the others' outside. This may arise whether or not there is an apparently natural geographical boundary, as in an island like ours. The up-side of such an ambition is the group cohesion it creates. The down-side of such nationalism is the powerful tendency to homogenise society and disregard the welfare of dissidents, and contribution of minority groups.

It is our view that the struggle between British and Irish nationalisms for control has tended to polarise our people, and to diminish the opportunity to recognise that many of us on this island do not wish to identify ourselves exclusively, or even primarily, with a British, Protestant, monarchical ethos, nor with a Gaelic, Roman Catholic, republican ethos. We come from many different roots, with diverse faiths, conflicting political creeds and rich cultural variety. The political task which lies ahead is for us to create structures which facilitate the expression and exchange of this rich diversity.

This by definition requires something much less tidy than the exclusivist propositions designed to give expression to Irish unity, or a simple United Kingdom.

PRINCIPLES UNDERLYING A RESOLUTION

We have earlier mentioned the principles of the Joint Declaration of 1993, and in our view these provide an excellent basis for progress. When combined with the widely accepted three sets of relationships, upon which, in recent years, talks have been based, a useful map emerges.

Firstly, it is for the people of Northern Ireland to find a way of living together, and deciding their own constitutional future. That we in Northern Ireland are divided in this is clear, so some other principles must be outlined to assist us in reaching agreement. Violence must not be regarded as a legitimate political instrument, and it is an enormous help in the search for a settlement that the use of terrorism has been set aside by both sides. It is also of central importance that the rights of every individual be respected and the contributions of all minorities be welcomed, facilitated and valued.

Secondly, whilst the people of Northern Ireland may for the present decide, for economic, social, historical and other reasons, to remain within the United Kingdom, the significance of our shared island home cannot continue to be minimised. The economic, environmental and social imperatives of cooperation can be ignored only at great cost to all of us. Structures within Northern Ireland must have institutional opportunities to work alongside the political arrangements in the Republic of Ireland. These institutions should express the realities of our relationships rather than a forced political agenda, so some may have more responsibilities than others, some may extend to the whole island, and others to this part or that. In all we should be striving to help relationships grow, rather than to force our people into fulfilling the requirements of a political creed.

Thirdly, the British and Irish Governments must deepen their mutual respect through constitutional expression. It would be counter-productive if the Irish Government sees it as important to address only the sensitivities of nationalists in the North, and the British Government is only really concerned about Northern unionists. Both Governments must be sensitive to the anxieties and aspirations of all sections of the people of Northern Ireland, and divorce themselves from any temptation to use partisanship as a card to be played in their own domestic politics, now or in the future.

Finally, we must all be prepared to pay a price for peace. An honourable compromise will require each side to give up exclusive rights, and elements of political control. London, Dublin, and our divided people must understand that there will not be mutual satisfaction without some sacrifice, but surely, after all this time, we have begun to realise the cost of failure, and to appreciate that the prize of peace is worth the price of peace.

DEMOCRATIC LEFT

THE NATURE OF THE PROBLEM

THE CONTEXT

PEOPLE MAY MAKE THEIR OWN HISTORY, but they do not do so in conditions of their own choosing. We in Democratic Left – as democrats and socialists – would not choose the circumstances that we are faced with in Northern Ireland. They are, however, the reality in which the people of Northern Ireland must make their history. In recognising this, we seek to show a way out of the nightmare of fear and hate. The real concerns of people – not just the concerns we believe they should have – must be taken on board.

What ultimately divides people in Northern Ireland is not religion, race, or ethnicity but national allegiance. Like any other society, there are many differences between people and groups in Northern Ireland. But the one difference which is at the heart of the instability, violence and terror is the division between the two, different national identities. National allegiance is at the core of the issue and history shows us that suppressing national identity is disastrous. Respect for, and valuing of, national identity within Northern Ireland is the first step towards reducing the political importance of these identities.

DOWNING STREET DECLARATION

The Downing Street Declaration recognises the legitimacy of Northern Ireland as part of the United Kingdom. It guarantees that its constitutional status can only change when a majority of its population wish it to change. Since the constitutional rights of a majority of people in Northern Ireland have therefore been recognised and are in the process of being acceded to, it is now time to formulate proposals for a truly democratic agreement which will also address the rights of the minority of nationalists in Northern Ireland. Such an agreement will require compromise within the Republic of Ireland, Northern Ireland, and between the British and Irish Governments.

HISTORICAL BACKGROUND

British nationality, or the 'imagined community' which is now the British nation, developed after the Revolution of 1688 and the Act of Union of 1707, and it developed in opposition to the threatening Catholic powers of Europe. It was a Protestant nationality with a Protestant monarchy, and it solidified during the eighteenth and nineteenth centuries on the basis of expanding trade and imperialism. It was the idea which united the culturally different countries of England, Scotland and Wales in one British nation.

Long after the more strident manifestations of British nationality and nationalism have declined in Wales, Scotland and England, the political discourse of eighteenth and nineteenth century Britishness is very much part of the political culture of Ulster unionists since they continue to be faced by the remnants of Catholic Europe, as they see it, in Ireland. The people in Northern Ireland who consider themselves as part of that British tradition must be accepted by Irish nationalists and others, as part of the British Nation and an agreement must recognise this fact.

Modern Irish nationality developed in the context of, and in opposition to, this powerful British identity. Nationalism has deep roots in Ireland. In the Republic these roots have been modified in the more confident Irish State in latter years. Traditional Irish nationalism, however, remains stronger among many in Northern Ireland. Any agreement must recognise this fact.

PRINCIPLES UNDERLYING A RESOLUTION

THE FUTURE

We in Democratic Left will seek to influence an agreement in such a way as to ensure that, in time, a politics develops in Northern Ireland where other identities such as class, gender, and political identity take precedence over national identities in determining political outcomes. We can do this by first recognising that the opposing national allegiances, which these identities can give rise to, have real meaning and importance for both groups. Since the right of the British-Irish is in the process of being conceded by Irish nationalism, it is time that the British State recognised that it has within its boundaries a sizeable proportion of people who do not subscribe to British nationality and whose national identity must be respected, officially recognised, and valued.

The seventy years separation from the South, the development of the welfare state, divergent social development North and South, and twenty five years of terrorism have made Northern nationalists a people apart. They have potentially more in common with their fellow Northern Irish people than with their Southern neighbours. The primary objective of an agreement should be to unite the people of Northern Ireland on the basis of peaceful co-existence by putting in place structures which will help develop a pluralist democracy.

WEIGHTED MAJORITY

As we point out later, we believe that an integral part of an agreement must be the establishment of a democratic assembly in Northern Ireland with legislative, budgetary and policing responsibilities. Given the history of Northern Ireland, however, and the nature of the divisions, there can be no question of simple majority rule. At the same time, power sharing on the basis of national allegiance would institutionalise divisions and make the emergence of a common identity more problematic.

Democratic Left, therefore, propose the concept of weighted majority decision-making at central and local levels in order to incorporate widespread community support for all major decisions. Weighted majority decision-making would mean, for example, that for all major decisions, particularly on sensitive issues, sixty or seventy per cent support would be required to carry a decision. The exercise of power would therefore require negotiation and agreement on issues relating, for instance, to policing. A minority of extremists undoubtedly would continue to have the capacity to make difficulties but they could not block progress. If the British State concedes structures where an Irish identity can be expressed by nationalists and valued in a manner that does not undermine their neighbours, the hold of extreme nationalism on the people will wane. If the British-Irish are given their security, extremes of loyalism will decline. Any agreement that does not recognise the potency of the dual nationalism will founder.

NATIONAL IDENTITY

An agreement must recognise that the community in Northern Ireland is divided in complex ways but primarily into two different national identities created by history.

An agreement must respect and value each nationality. The Republic must recognise the British national identity of the majority and the British State must recognise the Irish national identity of the minority.

National identity is not immutable and can and does change over time. The agreement must allow for this change, but not presuppose its direction, be that towards greater identification with Britain, with the Republic, or with Europe as a whole; or towards an indigenous Northern Ireland identity. The agreement therefore must provide for minorities of all kinds as well as majorities.

Currently, both national groupings in the North feel they are under attack and so at present the expression of nationality is in some cases extreme, reactionary, and violent. The agreement must allow for – and encourage – a more benign and positive expression of nationality.

We must seek to ensure that the struggle between the nationalities in Northern Ireland is replaced by a more productive and progressive expression of nationality, as occurs in societies where nationality is not under pressure or attack.

The means

Britain should legally recognise the existence of a significant national minority – the Irish of Northern Ireland – within the British State who do not subscribe to British nationality. Their rights, values, aspirations and culture should be legally recognised, respected and valued by the State.

The Republic of Ireland should amend Articles 2 and 3 of its Constitution:

(i) to convert the current territorial claim into an aspiration for the unity of people in Ireland;

(ii) to recognise Northern Ireland as part of the United Kingdom;

(iii) to recognise the existence and rights of the British-Irish and Irish nationalists in Northern Ireland;

(iv) to incorporate also the principle of consent to future constitutional change.

CIVIL RIGHTS

The recent conflict developed out of a demand for Civil Rights which arose from fifty years of discrimination in jobs, housing and electoral gerrymandering. The violent response to those demands enabled the IRA to push that campaign aside and pursue, through violence, traditional Republican objectives. The twenty five years of war waged by the IRA have not diminished the legitimacy of the original Civil Rights demands for protection of individual rights against arbitrary State power or against discrimination on the basis of religion or national allegiance.

A new constitutional framework for Northern Ireland must contain cast-iron legal protection of these rights which can be tested in court.

The means

A Bill of Rights for Northern Ireland should be specifically drafted to meet the concerns of all sections of the community. The provisions must be compatible with the more general requirements of international Human Rights Conventions.

The European Convention on Human Rights should be incorporated into the law of the United Kingdom and the Republic of Ireland, and into a newly agreed constitutional framework for Northern Ireland.

Within the new constitutional framework the Northern Ireland Constitution Act 1973, could be extended to cover indirect discrimination, as recommended by the Standing Advisory Commission on Human Rights in Northern Ireland, to require effective legislation to be maintained against discrimination by larger employers in the private sector.

Provision should be made for measures designed to improve the position of disadvantaged groups and to encourage greater integration of the two main sections of the community, notably in education and housing.

COMMUNAL RIGHTS

Measures against discrimination, however effective, may not always be sufficient to protect communities', as opposed to individuals', interests.

The Standing Advisory Commission on Human Rights for Northern Ireland has already recommended that the Northern Ireland Constitution Act should be amended to impose a specific duty on all public bodies to give equal value and esteem to the 'two major communities' in Northern Ireland.

In the context of a new constitutional framework incorporating a Bill of Rights, the formulations of international agreements, such as (1) the UN Declaration on the Rights of Persons belonging to national, ethnic, religious and linguistic minorities; (2) The European Charter for Regional and Minority Languages; and (3) the document of the Copenhagen meeting of the CSCE, could be used to give specific protection to community rights in such areas as education, culture and language.

EMERGENCY LAWS

There should be no derogation from the provisions of the European Convention on Human Rights in the event of an emergency (such as continuing serious paramilitary violence on one side or another). Members in all sections of the community would want to have a guarantee that oppressive measures could not be introduced or operated in a one-sided or abusive manner. Where such emergency powers are deemed necessary they should not be introduced except:

(i) By weighted majority vote in a Northern Ireland Assembly;

(ii) With the explicit provision for the involvement of international monitors in the operation of any emergency powers.

RIGHTS GUARANTEED BY REFERENDUM

In order to entrench a new Northern Ireland Constitution and Bill of Rights it would be important that they would be endorsed by a local referendum. This would make it extremely difficult for a future British Government to repeal the Bill of Rights without the consent of the people of Northern Ireland.

The new Northern Ireland Constitution incorporating the Bill of Rights could be incorporated into a new British-Irish agreement so that any subsequent amendment or appeal without the consent of both Governments would be a breach of the treaty, and could be challenged through the International Court of Justice.

The Council of Europe could be invited to play a more active role in helping to guarantee and adjudicate on individual and communal rights aspects of an agreement.

THE STRUCTURES

Northern Ireland has suffered greatly by being governed by unaccountable Ministers from Westminster, by quangos and by bureaucrats. There is a need for devolution, under the principle of subsidiarity, with powers being devolved to the lowest level practicable. Powers should be retained at Westminster and at regional level only where absolutely necessary.

Proposals which would provide for voluntary coalitions within a Northern Ireland assembly should be enacted, provided that the weighted majority principle is incorporated. However, we will not support a mandatory power-sharing assembly based on national identity and/or religious head counts since such an institution would freeze politics along present lines in perpetuity and make very difficult the emergence of normal democratic politics.

A Northern Ireland assembly should have legislative, budgetary and policing responsibilities. The devolution of such powers should depend upon the willingness to operate the weighted majority system. The devolution of powers to subsidiary elected bodies should carry the same condition. This would protect minorities while allowing for the development of normal politics.

The means

(i) The devolution of powers to a Northern Ireland assembly elected by proportional representation.

(ii) Powers to be devolved would depend upon prior agreement concerning the use of weighted majority in decision-making.

(iii) Decision-making on the basis of a weighted majorities system to be instituted at all levels in specified circumstances.

(iv) The devolution of all practical powers to regional and local councils on the same basis.

POLICING AND JUDICIAL SYSTEM

For the success of any agreement, policing must be fair – and be seen to be fair. The name RUC should be replaced by the Northern Ireland Police Service. Responsibility for policing should be devolved to a Northern Ireland assembly. Policing policy must be subject to weighted majority decision-making. The police service should be accountable to the general public, for instance by extending the Police Liaison Committees currently in existence in some areas and broadening the representation on the Police Authority. Police should also be accountable at Divisional level in order to reflect the make-up of various communities. An agreement should provide for measures including the Diplock Courts and the Prevention of Terrorism Act to be scrapped.

The means

(i) A reconstituted, unarmed police force to be known as the Northern Ireland Police Service.

(ii) Policing to be the responsibility of the Northern Ireland assembly under a weighted majority decision-making system.

(iii) The police to be publicly accountable at central and divisional level.

(iv) An agreement should provide for special powers to be repealed.

THE WIDER DIMENSION

An internal solution in Northern Ireland is no longer sufficient. Northern Ireland is part of the island of Ireland. Britain is geographically and historically the nearest neighbour of both parts of the island. Both Britain and Ireland are part of the European Union. The agreement must reflect these realities. This cannot be done, however, through joint sovereignty. The concept of joint sovereignty as applied to Northern Ireland is based on elitist, anti-democratic and sectarian assumptions about nationalists and unionists in Northern Ireland which at best would deadlock the situation and at worst intensify communal conflict.

The means

(i) Co-operation between North and South should be encouraged in those areas of mutual interest on the basis of joint boards of equal representation from North and South, to be responsible to democratically-elected bodies in Northern Ireland and the Republic.

(ii) British-Irish co-operation should be further developed through the British-Irish Parliamentary Body which should include members of a Northern Ireland assembly.

(iii) The Republic and Northern Ireland should relate to the EU jointly where it is in the interest of both to do so.

CONCLUSION

People not only have national identities – they have class, gender, regional, local, religious, sporting, occupational and other interlocking and diverse identities. We should try to make national identity just one other enriching aspect of people's lives – not a bigoted, fascist ideology that drives people apart.

National identity is not immutable. It does change. In today's world it is changing very fast. The 'imagined community' which is the Irish nation extends far beyond the borders of the Irish State and Northern

Ireland and includes English men playing soccer and rugby for Ireland. It includes, in part, the Irish diaspora in the UK, America and Australia. British nationality is also under pressure with the decline of Empire, while the re-emergence of a confident Scottish and Welsh identity may, in the future, transform it beyond recognition. We recognise that there are many people who do not subscribe to either of the two main national identities.

The reactionary, backward-looking remnants of old-style British and Irish nationalism, which confront each other in Northern Ireland and have the allegiance of many Catholic and Protestant people, must be overcome by addressing real fears and by respecting and valuing difference.

An agreement is needed, therefore, which is based on the democratic principle of consent; which provides a framework for the development of an open, civil society capable of accommodating differences through democratic politics and which avoids locking people into blocs based on religion or national identity.

In such circumstances, everyone could pursue their legitimate aspirations for a better society without threatening anyone else's sense of security or identity.

SENATOR GORDON WILSON

A T THE OUTSET LET ME SAY that I do not represent any Party, organisation or creed here. If I seem to emphasise the personal pronoun that is because I am here as an individual member of the Forum . While I lay no claim to represent anyone but myself, my words may reflect the views of some people in Northern Ireland.

I often regret that as a young man I did not stand up and speak out against injustice and wrong when I saw them happening in my part of the world. I drew back because I regarded politicians as hard men and I stayed comfortable. Now I hope that my words may help to soften our hearts and change the attitudes which fostered that injustice and the long years of violence in our corner of God's garden.

THE NATURE OF THE PROBLEM

I do not intend to give a long historical analysis of the problem in Northern Ireland. Many historians and political commentators have done that already. Perhaps what I can do is give a layman's view of the problem, a view which others like me may relate to. There are two main elements in the problem of Northern Ireland, a clash of cultures and a crisis of trust. And there are several related issues which complicate the problem.

CLASH OF CULTURES

Religion more than politics colours the thinking of the people in Northern Ireland. The British culture is part of the heritage of the Protestant community. The Irish culture is allied predominantly to the Catholic community. (When I use the term Catholic here I am in every case referring to the Roman Catholic church.) This has led to the dangerous stereotyping of Protestant as British and Catholic as Irish. It is not totally true, but there is enough truth in it to make it acceptable to many on and beyond this island. As so often here, the perception is more powerful than the reality. There has been a history of ascendancy, dominance and intolerance on both sides of that divide.

CRISIS OF TRUST

It is not popular to state, and it is often papered over, that people here do not trust one another. The basis of any lasting relationship is trust. Where that no longer exists there is little or no possibility of forming a stable society.

UNITED IRELAND

The great majority of the three quarters of a million Protestant people in Northern Ireland want to be British not Irish. Ninety five percent of them, if asked, would deny their Irishness. They are happy to describe themselves as Ulstermen or Tyronemen or Belfastmen but they believe that to call themselves Irish would be the first step towards acknowledging the possibility of a united Ireland. There is no doubt that in the minds of many of the unionist and Protestant people in Northern Ireland the road to a united Ireland is the road to Rome. Their greatest fear is that they will be swallowed up by Catholicism. They know that in the past the Catholic church has played a significant part in affairs of State in the Republic.

To those people I would like to say here that from my unique position as a Senator in the Irish Parliament for the past two years I have not seen any direct evidence of an input from the Catholic church in affairs of State. I am aware too that the Irish Government has passed some laws which do not conform to the teaching of the Catholic church.

Within the Northern Irish Catholic community there are a growing number of 'comfortable' people who do not want to break from Britain. In my opinion they know that a united Ireland cannot provide the economic advantages they enjoy under the present administration.

HEADS AND HEARTS

North and South, there is another division that we cannot ignore : the gap between head and heart. The heads of many of these 'comfortable' Catholics say that they are better off in Britain but when they get into a polling booth their hearts may hanker for old Ireland. Equally, there are Catholics in the South who do not want to know about a united Ireland largely for two reasons. One, because it would create a twenty five percent minority which would be difficult to control, and, two, because the Republic cannot afford it. But in the polling booth they too may feel the pull of old Ireland.

UNEMPLOYMENT

This is a major problem in this country, both North and South, and will remain so for a long time. Indeed, there are some who say that it will get worse in a less labour-intensive economy. Perhaps we need to be more honest with people, particularly with the young, and to admit that it is no longer possible for all to have employment. Such people have their pride too and need to feel that they are not regarded as second-class citizens, and need to be constantly reminded that the Government of the day cares for them.

THE RUC

Again, perception is important here. It is not my job to defend the RUC but I believe that it is the victim of misperception. It is regarded by many as a Protestant force, rather than a service, which is for Protestant people and which is anti-Catholic. The reality is that most law-abiding citizens feel satisfied with the service they get from the RUC.

Of course the RUC has made mistakes. Nevertheless, it has, in my opinion, done a very good job under enormous terrorist pressure.

Hundreds of its members have lost their lives in defending all of the people of Northern Ireland. The RUC barracks look like fortresses because they have been under consistent attack from the IRA.

PRINCIPLES UNDERLYING A RESOLUTION

We should make haste slowly. I said this at the inaugural meeting of the Forum and I think it bears repetition. Peace does come 'dropping slow' and the problems of four hundred years will not be solved in three months or maybe even in three years. We must be patient and persevere.

The Framework Document from the British and Irish Governments will be a crucial influence on the work of the Forum. Its proposals will, hopefully, help to concentrate our minds and sharpen the focus of our debate.

I believe firmly that one day a united Ireland will come. Indeed, the former Taoiseach said that he could not see it coming in his lifetime. Many unionists and Protestants in Northern Ireland welcomed that statement because it removed their fear that they would be attacked overnight and dragged into a united Ireland against their wishes.

In the meantime, politicians must decide on a form of government which will be fair, and which will be seen to be fair, and to which all the people of Northern Ireland can be loyal. They must devise an interim structure or administration on the way to a united Ireland. It seems to me that the Irish Government has a responsibility to persuade the unionist and Protestant people of Northern Ireland that their best future is in a united Ireland. This will not be easy but it must be done.

REFERENDUM

I have not met anybody in my province who does not want peace. The people of Northern Ireland must be consulted in a referendum simultaneous to, but separate from, that conducted in the Republic of Ireland. So far, all the delegations here, with the exception of Sinn Féin, have said this. It is a right which cannot be denied to the people of Northern Ireland who, whatever the future may hold, live today in the territory comprising the six counties and governed by Britain, which is the sovereign power.

UNITED IRELAND

Most of my friends, who are moderate people, do not want to know about a united Ireland. This is true of the majority of unionists and Protestant people. They do not want any constitutional interference by the Irish Government in their lives, but they could live with cross-border institutions based on common interests and I would encourage more efforts of this kind. There are already examples of this cooperation which are proving successful.

Most important of all, we need to cross the borders that exist within Northern Ireland and to develop more initiatives which will bring the two communities together. This is especially important for young people. I have seen the fruits of such exercises in the form of the Spirit of Enniskillen Bursary Award Scheme which covers both communities across the province and is one of the best exercises, if not perhaps the best, in community relations that exists today, but it is open to only fifty young people per year. Therefore, I feel we need to look at developing fully the scheme entitled Education for Mutual Understanding, now known as the Cross-Community Contact Scheme, which is open to all schools in Northern Ireland and affords far greater opportunities for children to learn from and about each other and to do away with some of the myths we have grown up with.

Integrated education of itself does not hold all the answers. The primary values are learnt at home and in the community. Parents need to learn to be open-minded. Likewise, the churches should look long and hard at the stances they take.

RUC

Much has been said during our debates about reform of the RUC, renaming the force, or creating two separate forces.

Change is beginning within the RUC. The Chief Constable is a Dublin man and several high-ranking officers are Catholics. There is already good communication at social and official level between the Gardaí and the RUC. Some members of the RUC would look kindly on a change of title but the unionists will not easily relinquish the royal connection.

As citizens we need to learn to trust and support our police. How can we expect others to protect us if we do not support them ? It is difficult for young Catholics to join an organisation they perceive as alien but they should be encouraged to do so. This will reassure the doubters that the RUC works for them too and that they will be treated justly.

EMPLOYMENT

We need to develop greater business cooperation between North and South and to handle carefully and skilfully the money we get from Europe and America. This should be used to enhance local industrial schemes rather than to assist multinational enterprises setting up here.

THREE RS

I believe that any hope for a resolution of the problem in Northern Ireland rests on three Rs : respect, resolve, reaching out.

Respect

To repeat the words I used in my submission to the Opsahl Commission: 'For too long people in Northern Ireland have been shouting when they should have been talking and talking when they should have been listening.' If our hearts and attitudes are to soften we must talk and, above all, listen to one another. By listening carefully , each side can learn to trust the other and to respect the other's point of view, even if they cannot agree with it.

It is strange that we who have such a reputation for accepting foreign visitors with warmth and friendship are unable to accept our neighbour's right to think differently from ourselves. We have to learn to accommodate the differences within our own society.

Resolve

For that respect and trust to grow, people on both sides of the border need to resolve to visit the other part of this island. I would encourage folk at every level to come North to meet people and to discover that the people of Northern Ireland are decent people, and vice versa. This can also be arranged on a semi-formal basis through schools, businesses and social clubs organising outings and exchange programmes. Again, it is strange that we send our children to France and Spain to learn languages but not to the other end of our own country to learn how their neighbours live.

Reaching Out

Although, at the end of the day, the politicians have to come up with a technical solution, the people on both sides of the community must reach out and share the very many things we hold in common. We can never agree on everything but let us at least agree to differ in peace. Let us learn to find a new way to live together based on the things we share, not least of which is the piece of earth we inhabit, and above all our common Maker.

Surely the human mind is wise enough, or there are men and women wise enough and with enough of the love of God in their hearts, to be able to find a solution for all the people in Northern Ireland. If it can happen, as it appears to be happening, that the South Africans, with their vast land and countless millions of people, can find a way forward, surely we, in our corner of God's garden, can find an answer to our problem.

CONCLUSION

To close I would like to quote the words of John Hewitt, an Ulster poet whose theme was the common heritage too easily and too often overlooked by the communities in Northern Ireland :

Speak peace and toleration. Moderate
your tone of voice, and everywhere avoid
what might provoke. Good will must be deployed
in efforts to restore our balanced state.
To long-held views sincere give proper weight;
one brief rash word and all might be destroyed.

MEMORANDUM FOR THE MODERATES

THE GREEN PARTY/COMHAONTAS GLAS

It is precisely because we believe that Opinion, and nothing but Opinion, can effect great permanent changes, that we ought to be careful to keep this most potent force honest, wholesome, fearless and independent.

JOHN MORLEY: *On Compromise.*

Tá an Comhaontas Glas den bharúil go gcaithfidh gach dream sa Tuaisceart meas a thabhairt do gach dream eile, an meas céanna ar mhaith leo a fháil ón dream eile. Is é seo eochair na síochána, agus caithfidh muid, – san Fhóram seo, agus taobh amuigh de, an eochair seo a chasadh.

Caisleán Bhaile Átha Cliath, Eanáir 1995

THE NATURE OF THE PROBLEM

POLITICAL ANALYSIS

THE PRIMARY POLITICAL CAUSE of the current Northern Ireland problem is the absence there of a consensus on the constitutional status, or the governance of the State.

This consensus has been absent at every stage in the development of the State from its inception.

A constitutional consensus is the norm in other democracies, and a pre-requisite for any State's claim to democratic status.

The exclusion of the minority, perceived by them as structural and permanent, undermined the legitimacy and stability of the State and led to violent resistance. The forced implementation of a majoritarian form of democracy in these circumstances amounted to institutional violence on the part of the State.

In Northern Ireland those who regarded themselves as Irish nationalists, who supported Home Rule and who considered themselves as a part of the Irish people as a whole on the island, were originally alienated by the violent process of the initial construction of the Northern Ireland State. This dissenting population, who then formed a substantial minority in the new State, were never thereafter encouraged to feel included in it. Their experience was that of second class citizenship. Northern Ireland was no closer to achieving a constitutional consensus by the time of the violent unionist response to the non-violent Civil Rights campaign in 1969 than it was at its foundation in 1920.

The internal conflict has been exacerbated by two external claims to the sovereignty of the State: the claim by the Government of Britain in the Government of Ireland Act, 1920, the Treaty of 1921 and the Ireland Act, 1949, and the de jure claim in the 1937 Free State Constitution.

Both of the communities in confrontation in Northern Ireland were committed to the majority rule, winner-takes-all approach to politics, and the state was enmeshed in a deadly zero sum game. Polarisation of both communities was inevitable and led to widespread abuses and discrimination both on the part of the State and of other agencies.

As a consequence of this, whilst the drafters of laws and of constitutions in Britain and Ireland concentrated upon the creation of institutions which emphasised our differences and difficulties, almost nothing was done to construct institutions which emphasised what we had in common, such as there has been, for instance, for the Benelux countries.

The first decision-making process to exacerbate alienation in Northern Ireland was the majority rule system and the prompt abandonment by Unionists of proportional representation in Parliamentary elections (specified in the 1920 Act). Some of those outraged by this process then resorted to an even worse decision-making process i.e the use of intermittent violence, at the cost of many lives. Both of these approaches are of the win-or-lose category: both tend to encourage, if not indeed force, people to take sides; and both allow the victor then to dominate the vanquished.

The stability other democracies enjoy derives primarily from the presence within them of a constitutional consensus on the nature of the State and its governance. It follows, as far as a political analysis can go, that the fundamental nature of the problem in Northern Ireland derives from its absence.

HISTORICAL BACKGROUND

This conflict has its roots in the centuries of conflict arising out of Gaelic Ireland's resistance to the English annexation of Ireland, and indeed some would argue that historical precedents for it go back much further. Be all that as it may, we shall concentrate here upon the events of the present century.

The partition of Ireland and the creation of the separate State of Northern Ireland came about as a result of a deep division within Ireland, a division brought about originally by England's imperialist policies in Ireland. In the early part of this century the Anglo-Irish conflict appeared to be moving towards a resolution with the drafting of the Home Rule Bill. However, this proved unacceptable to the unionist/British community, and a course of armed rebellion to frustrate Home Rule was embarked upon. Under the threat of unionist violence and in view of the outbreak of the First World War, the Home Rule Act was suspended, and never came into effect.

The crude compromise that was the 1921 Treaty, even if the legislation and Articles of the Treaty and the Government of Ireland Act had been fully honoured regarding the Boundary Commission, Proportional Representation and a Council of Ireland, created in Northern Ireland a State hopelessly devoid of the type of constitutional consensus that underpins the stability of democratic States. For the island as a whole it created two mutually antagonistic States defined in all but name along sectarian lines.

This institutionalised divide was detrimental to the development of both States. For the Protestants of the Republic the experience was one of exclusion and decline as their numbers dwindled, whilst their relative economic strength buttressed them from any worse effects. For the proportionally larger Catholic population of Northern Ireland the sense of grievance was greater, not only because of the very significant demographic differences between their situation and the Protestants in the Free State but also because of their sense of betrayal as part of the national majority sacrificed to accommodate what they saw as the national minority. Their sense of alienation was further intensified by their weaker economic position vis a vis the majority population in Northern Ireland.

There are lessons in this for us all when devising systems based upon the 'parity of esteem' principle. All need to be mindful when advocating models not to repeat the errors of the past by constructing systems which institutionalise the divide, such as happened in Bosnia, contributing towards the outbreak of civil war in that country.

The Free State, with its greater level of consensus and the relative economic strength of its minority, grew to enjoy a great degree of stability. Nevertheless, it must be said it did little if anything during its first fifty years of life to allay Northern unionists' fears that 'Home Rule is Rome Rule'. On the contrary, from the enactment of the Constitution in 1937, through the Mother and Child debacle in 1951 to the more recent divorce referendum it enacted a raft of social legislation reflecting a largely Roman Catholic ethos.

The Northern Ireland State, dubbed a 'Protestant Parliament for a Protestant people' by its Premier, developed into a single-Party State, operating through its own brand of sectarian domination. The resulting experience of the Irish nationalist, predominantly Roman Catholic population, was one of exclusion and discrimination, generally perceived as tolerated if not indeed initiated by the State itself.

Normal politics could not develop in this situation, neither within the institutions of the State nor in society at large. When in the late 1960s the Civil Rights movement attempted to redress these grievances through non-sectarian and non-violent agitation the response was a pogrom with mob attacks and the burning of hundreds of houses. An historic opportunity to build a consensus was lost, and as Northern Ireland was pulled downward into a violent vortex the Civil Rights movement all but disappeared and the old conflict, predicated upon the war between Irish separatism and the British State in Ireland, was reborn.

The deadly and stalemated endgame between the two forces required acts of generosity and trust to alter the political landscape and to give peace a real chance. On 1 September 1994 the Republican movement made one such gesture, and, following the Loyalist ceasefires, an historic opportunity was created to construct in Northern Ireland, in the whole of Ireland, and within these islands, a true political consensus, founded not upon the sovereignty of monarchs, nations or Governments, but upon the pooled sovereignty of individuals.

PRINCIPLES UNDERLYING A RESOLUTION

The Green principles that guide our approach to the Northern Ireland problem derive from what is a central principle of political ecology worldwide i.e. non-violence. Non-violence involves far more than a simple laying down of arms. It is a science, with its own rationale, its own pedagogy and its own techniques. It has implications not alone for forms of Government but also for the means by which forms of Government are agreed, indeed it has implications not alone for the means by which they are agreed but for the very language to be used to this end.

Most relevant to the Northern Ireland situation are the Green principles of anti-imperialism and post-nationalism, the one emphasising the rights of small nations subsumed by force into larger entities, the other critical of the nation State, defined as national groups occupying territory on an exclusivist basis, subsuming their minorities with centralist authority. In differing ways Green philosophy therefore has relevance to the arguments of both Irish traditions, favouring a radically de-centralised polity with local, regional, national, continental and global tiers of administration, with decision-making taken at the most locally effective level. It is possible for Northern Ireland to construct such a polity for itself, in agreement, offering itself as a model region for a Europe of the regions within the European Union wherein sovereignty will be shared and national and regional identities will be able to exist in the same territories.

In common with our sister Green Parties in Northern Ireland, Scotland, England and Wales we stress the need for an international dimension and involvement in the peace process both

to give effect to the international community's responsibility and
to provide a neutral input to the process itself. Furthermore, we would
stress that the Green economic policies of greater self-reliance and
of international community-led cooperation in environmental
protection (e.g. THORP) would in themselves greatly assist the healing
process.

The following principles must, in our view, underly any settlement
agreed by the people of Northern Ireland, and are informed by the above
outlined joint focus of all of the Green Parties of these islands.

THE PRINCIPLES

Compromise

An inclusive settlement that has the support and agreement of all
groups, within the Northern Ireland area, within all of Ireland and
between all of us on these islands, is the only settlement that will work.
It follows that a decision-making process that allows for compromise
will be critical to that process.

Constitutional balance

There is no consensus in Northern Ireland for a united Irish Republic.
Equally, there is no consensus for a purely internal settlement within the
United Kingdom. Somewhere between these extremes there exist the
parameters of a consensus. It is important that this reality is reflected in
the forthcoming Joint Framework Document and that there are no
plans within it for unilateral constitutional change either for Ireland or
for the United Kingdom, but that both Ireland and the United
Kingdom would undertake to accept and legislate for the consensus
which emerged in Northern Ireland.

No coercion

The coercion of unionists into a United Ireland cannot form any part
of an agreed settlement and likewise nor can the continued coercion of
Northern nationalists into the United Kingdom.

Consent

As a matter of practicality no major change in the constitutional status
of Northern Ireland can come about without the consensual agreement
of its people.

Constitutional change

A new constitutional arrangement will be at the heart of any agreed settlement. It must be based upon the highest degree of consensus arrived at through negotiation and voting with the use of consensual techniques such as the preferendum (see appendix).

Non-violence and de-militarisation

This can be achieved only through a non-violent process, which, as well as requiring the ending of paramilitary violence, requires the full de-militarisation of society. In practical terms for Northern Ireland this means the return of all troops to barracks and their subsequent standing down or withdrawal from Northern Ireland. It further requires the normalisation of the judicial process and ultimately the complete de-commissioning of paramilitary weapons and the huge number of legally held firearms. We further perceive the long-term need for local community-based police who have the respect of the whole local population and who do not carry arms. Policing methods and organisation should be reviewed to enhance the prospect of cross-community support. Common standards of policing should apply on the model of the forty one constabulary committees in the United Kingdom. In the interim the RUC should immediately cease to carry weapons.

Bill of Rights

Interim measures will be required both to consolidate the peace and to move the process on. These would include the passing into law of a Bill of Rights and the involvement of international observers of the peace, and particularly of security matters in this interim.

Post-nationalist anti-imperialism

Given that Northern Ireland is an area occupied by differing groups of people of differing national allegiances, it follows that any agreed polity would both reflect and value this diversity and no longer offer them as mutually exclusive alternatives. As there may be need to give a territorial definition to this reality there must be no bar to Northern Ireland defining itself within a model that goes beyond the limits of the nation State, allowing for models such as joint authority, confederation, cantonisation and federation to be considered.

Separation of church and State

The full separation of church and State, i.e. all churches and all States party to the conflict, together with the encouragement of non-denominational and multi-denominational education (without affecting the rights of parents to choose a denominational education for their children), together with the provision of a pluralist school curriculum which values equally all the various cultural strands that make up a society will be an important aspect in any agreed settlement.

Parity of esteem

Any political proposals to end the current political conflicts in Northern Ireland should be based, then, not upon victory of any one of the parties to the conflict, but upon a polity which recognises the common dependence of each and the need for each to extend total parity of esteem to each other. It is a challenge, but one which can be overcome, for a system to be devised whereunder individual and joint British-Irish citizenship can be recognised and flourish. It follows that parity of esteem should extend to both the Irish and the English languages.

THE PRINCIPLES UNDERLYING THE METHODOLOGY OF REACHING A SOLUTION

The construction of a consensus

If the fundamental problem is the absence of a constitutional consensus it follows that the fundamental work of those working towards the resolution of the problem will be the creation of a *methodology* to achieve such a consensus. The methodology proposed by the two Governments involves a series of talks, presumably bilateral at first, between the mandated political Parties in the North and the British Government. These would lead to round table talks leading on to all-Party talks involving the Irish Government. When all-Party agreement is reached concurrent referenda would be held in both jurisdictions. Whilst the Green Party would of course cooperate with such an approach, and whilst we would support any agreed settlement that might emerge from it, we would here point out what we see as the weaknesses of such an approach and suggest improvements.

The principal flaw in this approach lies in its near total dependence upon the political Parties as the main instruments for achieving a consensus. Political parties are designed to function within an adversarial context and may prove unable to make the adjustments necessary to convert themselves into 'the engines for consensus'. The British Government, implicitly recognising this, are suggesting that in the event of a breakdown *they alone* would present their own proposals to the people of Northern Ireland. This is a very high-risk strategy and one that we believe is democratically flawed. As the only democratically-mandated organisations involved in the conflict the Parties will of course have a central role to play, however, it is the Green Party's view that sovereignty derives not from political Parties, nor from Governments nor nations but in the final analysis *from individuals*. Below we outline a methodology that takes this into account.

An open constitutional conference should be initiated, made up of elected representatives elected by PR-STV in seventeen five-member constituencies. A number of additional members should be elected on the following criterion: for each two percent of the overall vote which each Party receives, that Party should get one elected representative. The conference would be open to proposals from church leaders, women's groups, community associations etc. All proceedings would be facilitated by independent facilitators and consensors chosen from abroad. The consensors would be charged with the task of drawing up a multiple choice referendum (preferendum see Appendix) offering a range of (perhaps ten) evenly balanced options, and these would then be voted on by the electorate. The proceedings of the conference should be broadcast.

CONCLUSION

In conclusion, let us summarise that the conflict in Northern Ireland has its roots in a centuries-old conflict which has involved all of these islands. In simple political terms the problem may be expressed as the absence of a constitutional consensus resulting in the exclusion and/or the withdrawal of one community from the State. It follows that the work of the peace process, in strictly political terms, must be the facilitation of the construction by the people of a true consensus. The above serves as a methodology to this end.

APPENDIX

THE PREFERENDUM – A SUMMARY

Under most electoral systems, be they majoritarian or proportional, the success of any one policy proposal or candidature depends on the views or votes of only a faction in society; and most voting systems (i.e., the decision-making procedures) are even worse, allowing as they do one faction to dominate the rest. Some win, and win everything, while others only lose.

In consensus systems, in contrast, the success of any one policy proposal or candidature depends not on the views of just a faction in society but on the views of everyone (who votes). So no one person or Party will win everything, but almost all participants will win something.

It should be stressed that consensus voting is not some mathematical concoction by which 'the silent majority' shall be better represented; rather, it is a methodology based on human rights. For no 'majority' has the 'right' to impose its views upon others, and no minority the 'right' of veto. Instead, we all have a responsibility to our neighbours. Accordingly, the democratic process should be a means by which is established 'the greatest good of the greatest possible number'. The majority vote, a comparative methodology, cannot reach this aspiration; but consensus voting facilitates exactly that.

The basic criteria are as follows:

1   Decide how many options best represent all proposals now 'on the table' and present a balanced list as a preferendum.

Accordingly, when it comes to the preferendum vote:

(i)   there shall always be at least 3, usually 5–10 options, and rarely more than 12;

(ii)   each voter – and let us assume the first one is a she – may vote for (most if not) all the options listed; thus, in a ballot, she should give 5 points to the option she likes the most, and she may give 4 to her second choice, 3 to her next preference... and so on, down to a 1 for the option she likes least of all.

The rules for partial voting are as follows: he who votes for only one option/candidate will exercise only 1 point; she who votes for two will exercise 2+1 = 3 points; he who votes for three will exercise 3+2+1 = 6 points, and so on; so only she who votes for all five will exercise the full 5+4+3+2+1 = 15 points; in other words, those who participate but partially in the democratic process shall exercise just a partial influence, and only those who participate fully shall exercise a full influence;

(iii) the count shall be conducted by adding all the points cast for each option. The option which achieves the highest number of points is the one with the highest level of consensus.

Full details may be found in:

P.J. EMERSON: *The Politics of Consensus* ISBN 0 9506028 4 1

INDEPENDENT DEPUTIES
IN DÁIL ÉIREANN

THE NATURE OF THE PROBLEM

THE INTERVENTION OF THE NEIGHBOURING ISLAND of Great Britain in Irish affairs has been disastrous for all parties concerned over many centuries. This fact must be acknowledged by all fair-minded and rational people.

THE IRISH

First of all, the native Irish always wished to rule themselves and through a long succession of military and constitutional methods have made efforts to detach themselves from Britain. These efforts have resulted in much hardship, many cruelties and deaths, as the British used repression to quench the intermittent rebellions and to systematically suppress independence movements.

THE BRITISH

Secondly, the British themselves (with England the controlling power) have always been resented in Ireland and have been the recipients of the reactive and secondary violence of the Irish in their efforts to dislodge them. This has resulted over time, in the British, particularly the English, perceiving the Irish as a lesser breed, a sort of *Untermenschen*, who must always be crushed with *cos ar bolg* action. A corollary of this attitude has been that severe damage has been done to the political fabric of British affairs and to her international reputation in that:

(i)   civil liberties have been curtailed

(ii)   massive emergency powers remain on the statute books

(iii)   the criminal justice system has been damaged as a result of a series of miscarriage of justice cases

(iv)   the police have fallen into disrepute

(v)   censorship and surveillance obtains.

THE PRO-UNION STOCK

They are primarily located in the north eastern part of Ireland – Antrim, East Derry, North Down and North Armagh. As a people, they have never addressed a *modus vivendi* with their fellow Irishmen, because the British were prepared to underwrite them economically and politically. They now live in an irrational *laager* world with fears of their own fellow Irish of paranoid dimensions and a fear of betrayal by the English of similar dimension. Because the State of Northern Ireland seems absolutely guaranteed by the British, no progressive forces have ever emerged among the unionists, and politics in the six counties are always dominated by the constitutional issue. Topics such as the Battle of the Boyne in 1690, triumphalism, sectarianism, coat-trailing of monarchical regalia and symbolism together with militarism are ever present.

PRINCIPLES UNDERLYING A RESOLUTION

The extent of the six county State is a gerrymander in that it incorporates the largest amount of territory consistent with the maintenance of a pro-union majority which has since been sought to be permanently retained by an all-pervasive discrimination against, and harassment of, its nationalist people. Britain must be made to realise and understand what it is still doing to Ireland by underwriting such a state of affairs. It is not just simply that Irish people are sundered from each other, but that the economy is similarly sundered. In the maintenance of this constitutional arrangement, (which, if measured equitably, is manifestly unfair to nationalists) much wasteful expenditure is incurred.

A large part of the GDP of the Republic and a considerable amount of UK Exchequer funding is needed to sustain the *status quo*. Incidentally, it is worth noting that the Irish taxpayer pays three times as much, on average, as his British counterpart for the maintenance of a border that the vast majority in Ireland do not want and cannot afford.

Britain should change its policy on Ireland in a radical way by a declaration of intent to withdraw politically from the island. The British should realise, as they must, that there are many forces at work within Ireland today which will mean that in the near future she will have to withdraw in any case. The main forces are:

Economic

The island is rapidly developing into one economy. The European experience will speed up the process further.

Demographic

The gap in the population of nationalists vis à vis unionists is closing despite the enforced emigration of an undue number of the nationalist people over the years. The latest census indicated 43:57. By the end of the century, even political control of Belfast may be lost by the unionists.

Administrative

Once again, with Europe leading the way, Ireland could usefully be administered as one unit. A small island of five million people does not need two bureaucracies and a duplication of distribution networks.

Social and cultural

More and more interaction – social, cultural and commercial – will inevitably take place between the two parts of Ireland. The main churches will become an increasingly unifying factor as also will the various sporting bodies which are organised on an all-Ireland basis.

Infrastructural

The road network when completed will help to knit and integrate the two parts of our island in a very material way. The Dublin–Belfast Corridor, when constructed, will be of immense benefit to the east coast and especially to our two main cities, the combined population of which is two million, representing forty percent of the entire population of the island. Likewise, we would sincerely hope that the construction of similar linkages between Dublin/Monaghan/Derry and Dublin/Cavan/Enniskillen would result in equivalent benefits to the north midlands and the north west.

CONCLUSION

Once the decision of Britain to withdraw from Ireland is accepted in principle, it seems right that the British be obliged to condition the unionists to the new situation and to become persuaders of the fact. Clearly this should be done in an enlightened and sensitive manner.

The last Forum which met in 1984 itemised and prioritised the options for us. They hold good today and a unitary state would rationally and logically be the most welcome outcome.

The removal of the unionist veto would unlock progressive forces which would give every hope that against a background of promised British withdrawal, a mutual, interim accommodation could be agreed between the communities in the Six Counties and between the peoples of the North and South.

Only then, would the Irish people enjoy full democracy and achieve their full potential.

INDEPENDENT SENATORS

THE NATURE OF THE PROBLEM

THE NATURE OF THE PROBLEM IN NORTHERN IRELAND is simplistically portrayed as the mutual suspicion of people of the Nationalist and Unionist Parties and the lack of cooperation between these two groups. Along with this, a substantial number of those who espouse the Unionist cause are not in favour of any cooperation with institutions in the Republic of Ireland.

There is, however, a large middle group of practical people who have straddled the middle ground in Northern Ireland and have brought about major initiatives to the benefit of both communities. These initiatives are often undertaken by women and it is worth noting that this Forum for Peace and Reconciliation has been a place where these women have been able to meet with politicians of all Parties in the Republic and many from Northern Ireland.

All the Independent Senators have had experience of cross-border initiatives or membership of cross-border organisations which have been mutually beneficial to both parts of the island. As has been pointed out in other submissions, there are all-island trade union organisations, sporting organisations and professional bodies. These have functioned successfully, usually without any animosity, between members from both parts of the island and it is this sort of cross-border, all island co-operation which we would like to see extended.

Cooperation exists between Government departments in Northern Ireland and the Republic in many areas but such cooperation should be considered the norm and could be set up between all departments with minimal expense or bureaucracy. Such cooperation exists in many parts of the world, for example, in the Nordic countries and in the Benelux countries.

PRINCIPLES UNDERLYING A RESOLUTION

Concentration on those in the middle ground in Northern Ireland is needed – so is concentration on all those areas where cross-border cooperation already exists.

Our objective is to find common ground in a context outside or transcending the traditional pigeonholes of religion, Party or even class. We believe that lack of participation in the political community and the workplace created the alienation which exploded into violence in 1969. We believe that this process needs to be reversed. We need to eliminate alienation in favour of participation. We, in the Independent Senators' Delegation, who have had experience in all the areas of education, medicine, business, trade unions and other fields, on an all-island basis, believe that our focus now as a Forum should be on the sub-political structures. We believe that there should be a common approach to problems, directing the resources throughout the island to solve our problems. Whether that be the sharing of artificial hips, third level places or fish is irrelevant but we must look at all sections and always in terms of gaining in the European context where we have common problems.

We believe, for instance, that the European requirement for getting the best for the whole island allowed under the Objective 1 conditions, could, by choice, be related either to the economic indicators of Dublin or the economic indicators of London, whichever best advantages the whole island. The expertise and commitment of professional, vocational and community leaders should be harnessed permanently to advance tolerance and pluralism. We need to find a way of selecting and involving in decision-making those people on a basis other than religion or Party or national identity.

THE WORKERS' PARTY

INTRODUCTION

ANY ANALYSIS OF NORTHERN IRELAND, its serious internal problems, its relationships with the Republic and the remainder of the United Kingdom must begin from a specific conceptual frame of reference, either stated or unstated. The Workers' Party perception derives from both the historic revolutionary, democratic tradition of the French Revolution brought to Ireland by Tone and the international socialist tradition encapsulated in the work and life of Connolly. Essentially our analysis derives solely from working class perspectives and interests as we understand them.

We wish also at this stage of our submission to remove any possible misunderstandings concerning the political aims of The Workers' Party. They are as follows:

> The Workers' Party long term goal is the establishment of a democratic, secular, socialist unitary state – a republic.
>
> .... To achieve this objective The Workers' Party will have won the support of the overwhelming majority of the working class in Northern Ireland and the Republic of Ireland. It cannot be achieved by coercion or subterfuge.
>
> THE CASE FOR DEVOLVED GOVERNMENT IN NORTHERN IRELAND P 2

The existence of two States North and South is a reality and they cannot be bombed out of existence or wished out of existence and the historical, cultural and religious differences which have given rise to the present situation,including the terror gangs, cannot be ignored.

(ibid.) p.3

Our position is therefore one which subscribes fully to the democratic, political decision-making process and at the same time recognises both States in Ireland as legitimate expressions of the democratic will of the majority of the citizens in each of the States.

THE NATURE OF THE PROBLEM

HISTORICAL MATERIAL CONTEXT OF THE PROBLEM

That there are a number of conflicting narratives of the period 1920 to 1994 is indicative of the problem of dealing with historical fact. Ruling out such monster descriptions which blame the condition of Northern Ireland entirely on the British or the unionists or the nationalists means that we are more likely to come to a version of history which will approximate closer to the truth. Needless to say this does not eliminate the possibility of serious disagreement of interpretation but it does have the virtue of raising the level of debate beyond the narrow sectarian confines within which it has traditionally taken place. The Workers' Party would argue that there are roughly three relatively distinct periods in the modern history of Northern Ireland:

1920–1945

This is characterised in the main by the consolidation of two all-class alliances which coexisted in uneasy, but profitable agreement, for the dominant elements. It is noticeable that both the Nationalist and Unionist groupings, in spite of Northern Ireland being heavily industrialised, were largely under the control of leaderships having strong rural roots and values which in effect meant that they were largely out of sympathy with the severe problems facing the urban working class. Residual aspects of this 'rural ideology' are still apparent in most of Northern Ireland's political Parties.

Certainly there were exceptions to this and undoubtedly Belfast played a role – in terms of progressive politics, largely negative – in both the Unionist and Nationalist programmes. However, in spite of the existence of a large working class, it could do little if anything to upset the existing alliances as events of the 'hungry '30s' demonstrated. The outbreak of the war against Fascism put local politics on hold, as it were, but it was to initiate dramatic changes in Northern Ireland which would continue until the events of 1969.

1945–1970

The impact of the Beveridge proposals on education and health introduced into Northern Ireland by the new British Labour Government elected in 1945 were to have profound and far-reaching effects on both the political and social structures of Northern Ireland. Unfortunately, not all of this development was progressive.

The subsequent expansion of third level education meant that access to higher education became available for the first time to a significant number of working class students.

In this context it is interesting to note that the student generation which became involved in civil rights activity in 1968-69 was roughly the first generation to be able to take advantage of the post-war education legislation.

Certainly there were exogenous factors influencing that dimension of events particularly Berkeley, California and Paris but in the main the developments of the late '60s were located in the emergence of the Northern Ireland Civil Rights Association (NICRA) and the decision of the then Republican movement to pursue political agitations instead of military campaigns.

Unfortunately the Unionist response was located in attitudes formed by events in the '20s, '40s and '50s when IRA campaigns of various duration seemed to pose a threat to the existence of the State. At the same time major industrial changes were taking place in Northern Ireland, particularly the virtually absolute decline of traditional industry accompanied by the growth of a strong anti-Unionist Party vote; the implications of this and the sociological changes mentioned above failed to impact on Unionist thinking. Two major misinterpretations of the

Civil Rights Campaign led to the communal violence of 1969; one was the Unionist leadership's belief that a major revolutionary conspiracy was taking place and their heavy-handed actions convinced the unionist population that this was the case. The statement from then Taoiseach Jack Lynch – 'we will not stand idly by' – reinforced this belief.

This is in no way to excuse the vicious barbaric assaults that took place on sections of the Roman Catholic population which aroused the justifiable fear that a province-wide pogrom was about to take place. Indeed in certain areas in Belfast a pogrom was attempted and thousands fled their homes. At the same time the violence shocked the British Government and, perhaps more importantly, established in the minds of the vast majority of the people of Northern Ireland that real changes would have to be introduced, politically, economically and socially. At no time, however, was the aim of NICRA to bring down Stormont as the seat of government.

The totality of subsequent progressive legislation, then, was a direct consequence of the NICRA campaign, namely, the reform of local government, the introduction of proportional representation in voting, the creation of the important Northern Ireland Housing Executive and measures to end discrimination in employment.

1970 to the present

In the aftermath of 1969 the British Government moved to create an unarmed police service and disbanded the B Specials. However, before the results of the Civil Rights Campaign could begin to penetrate the Northern Ireland social system and create an impetus for ongoing pervasive democratisation of society the police were rearmed. This was done in circumstances where it was clear that a nationalist terrorist campaign was being mounted, based on the impact of the communal violence of 1969.

There can be no doubt that support from elements in Fianna Fáil, at a time when that Party was in Government, played a major role in 'legitimising' the activities of the Provisional IRA. This was reinforced by right-wing Irish-American material support and, paradoxically, by far left elements in Britain and on the Continent.

The base for a 'freedom struggle' was further enhanced by the crassness of the British Government at the behest of the Unionist leadership – the Falls Road curfew in 1970, the introduction of internment in 1971 and the killings of Bloody Sunday in 1972. At the same time Provisional violence fuelled the development of loyalist terror gangs so that the stage was set for the involvement of growing numbers in sectarian Nationalist and Loyalist terrorist organisations and the consequent horrific list of tragedies of the past twenty four years.

There is a critical aspect of this period which requires special mention and that is the collapse of the Northern Ireland Labour Party (NILP) during the initial years of sectarian violence. There can be no doubt that the murderous actions of the Nationalist and Loyalist terrorist organisations were a major factor in bringing this about. Workers, who formed the vast majority of NILP voters, were driven by fear, to retreat from 'left' politics into traditional Orange and Green camps.

The Workers' Party (then Sinn Féin) realised in 1972 that the outcome of the growing violence would be the sectarian polarisation of Northern Ireland and a retreat from progressive political development. We condemned and opposed all acts of terrorism then as we do now.

Our political activity over these two decades has been to pursue the goals of peace, work, democracy and class politics. The proposals which we now put forward still have those perspectives in view.

PRINCIPLES UNDERLYING A RESOLUTION

The most enduring guarantee of peace in Northern Ireland would be agreement between the political Parties that the basis for progress is the total and unconditional acceptance of the democratic principle. It is hard to see in the absence of such a democratic consensus how we can go beyond the present type of discussion taking place within this Forum, valuable as it is.

The Workers' Party cannot accept that abiding fully by the democratic principle in any way militates against the political pursuit of either Unionist or Nationalist political objectives. At the same time we appreciate the fears that such a statement may create in the minds of those belonging to minority Parties, therefore we argue that a Bill of Rights (our proposals are with the Forum secretariat and the Northern Ireland Office) is essential to political progress in Northern Ireland.

Such a Bill of Rights would go a long way to solving problems relating to the policing of the State. Clearly, a Bill of Rights is not a panacea but it would lay down the democratic political parameters within which political progress can be made and at the same time perform an important social psychological function in relation to the exercise of State powers. Equally, a Bill of Rights would play a critical role in the future of a new Northern Ireland devolved government.

The establishment of fresh democratic institutions is absolutely central to the resolution of the vast range of problems which we face, from unemployment to the serious tackling of the vicious sectarian division in the community. At the same time genuine and positive North-South relations could only emerge when these institutions are in place. The Workers' Party over the years has supported the notion of bilateral boards in areas where there is clear agreement that this would be to the advantage of the people; some suggest themselves automatically – tourism, agriculture, transport, power; others could be, but not necessarily so, more contentious – investment, job creation and European relations.

CONCLUSION

We are convinced that the vast majority of people in Ireland desire solutions somewhere along the lines that we propose. They want peace and politics not violence and sectarianism; they want a society or societies in which their children can create a world in which they will have work, education, decent homes and provision for their old age. In other words they want an Ireland free from the social, political and economic evils which have for too long dominated all our lives.

RESPONSES

to

A NEW FRAMEWORK
FOR AGREEMENT

CONTRIBUTIONS BY FORUM
DELEGATIONS TO A DEBATE ON THE
FRAMEWORK DOCUMENT

FIANNA FÁIL

W E ARE VERY GLAD OF THE OPPORTUNITY to reiterate and to amplify our position on the Framework Document. And indeed we have listened with great interest to what the Tánaiste has had to say. We welcome without qualification the Framework Document. As you know, we were involved in it to a considerable extent and it has reached a most satisfactory conclusion. Indeed, I think we should acknowledge that the British Government have also shown real commitment to it, even at some particular political cost, I think, to themselves.

We view it as neither a rigid blueprint nor as a simple discussion document. The Framework Document is essentially the agreed negotiating position of both Governments. Throwing the document away will not alter the fact that the Governments have taken a considered view of some of the key issues. Those issues, such as the North-South relationship, will not simply go away, even though the Document may in the beginning seem to be ignored by some people.

Equality campaigners in the North are satisfied with the language in the appropriate documentation about equality and parity of esteem. The real challenge will be how to take it forward from here. Internal arrangements for the North are primarily for the Parties there, but fairness and partnership are the relevant principles. We are satisfied with the balance on constitutional issues which is consistent with the position we had negotiated.

The British accept that the Government of Ireland Act of 1920 must be replaced or amended and that the future will be vested irrevocably in the people of the North. In conformity with the renunciation by the British Government in the Joint Declaration of any selfish, strategic or economic interest in Northern Ireland, any territorial claim to sovereignty will be removed.

We recently had here a very interesting contribution by Pieter Dankert, the former President of the European Parliament and, indeed, a former Dutch Minister. He spoke of the need for a triple equality in a divided community – equal rights, equal opportunity and equal treatment. We would like to see those three principles contained in any new agreement as a concrete expression of parity of esteem.

The Joint Framework Document proposes three elements as the outline of a peace settlement. These are: the restoration of internal political institutions in the North on a consensual basis; the establishment of a North-South link in areas of mutual interest; and balanced constitutional change which removes any imposed or perceived threat of coercion. Whether or not there will be a united Ireland sometime in the future will be for the people of Ireland, North and South, to decide freely and concurrently. The development of inclusive negotiations around these issues would give an enormous boost to confidence in the permanence and durability of the peace process. This offers an unique opportunity, particularly for the people of Northern Ireland, to break out of the prison of history.

The political history of the stage we have now reached is of some substance. We, in the Fianna Fáil Party, congratulate the Taoiseach, the Tánaiste and the Government for what they have done in this regard. And may I say, as a delegate to this Forum, that I think the Forum for Peace and Reconciliation has played a very important role. I hope it will continue to do so.

We have had a sequence of events, each one seemingly compartmentalised but not really so. We have had the talks leading up to the Downing Street Declaration, the launching of the Declaration talks leading to the ceasefires on both sides, and now the Framework Document.

The setting up of this Forum has been strongly interlinked with all of the earlier events. The aims and objectives which the Delegations have set out provide a solid base for the Forum's work. The Tanaiste's call to the Unionists here today was delivered in a generous and open way. It is a call that I hope will receive a response. I know that you, Chairperson and your Secretariat have been particularly keen that we would draw Unionists into this process. In many ways, the voice of Unionists, even if not directly represented here, is represented, perhaps, in the presentations of various Delegations who have come here. The work we are doing here needs to be made better known outside, and I think that is happening. I think the peace process itself has now entered its political phase. From now on, it is its forward movement that counts.

The whole situation has now been infused with a momentum which, I hope, cannot and should not cease. Whilst we recognise and praise the Framework Document, inherent in this is the need for further movement. There should be no full stop at any stage of this process. In very simple terms, people in the North now have a chance to live their lives in a full fashion again. It is for all of us to explore how we can move forward into an inclusive political process.

THE SOCIAL DEMOCRATIC AND LABOUR PARTY

THE SDLP WELCOME THE FRAMEWORK DOCUMENT as an aid to discussion, i.e. in the terms in which it has been offered. Indeed, in the terms in which it was first asked for by others. We want to acknowledge the commitment, insight and sheer hard work that went into its preparation in circumstances that were often adverse and indeed perverse.

Given the nature of the document and the stated positions of others, it would not be polite for us at this point or in this Forum – to make detailed comments or take fixed positions on any of the arrangements or institutions indicated in its prospectus.

We can record our encouragement that the document clearly affirms the need for effective and relevant arrangements to address and accommodate each of the three sets of relationships which are involved in the problem we are working to solve. Others have agreed with us before this that those three sets of relationships form the scope of the problem and so must also be the scope of any solution. We have noted Unionists' objections to the possible scale or shape of given arrangements but we have not noted an unambiguous affirmation on their required scope.

Other documents have been published as well. These may not impress us particularly but we have not dismissed, discounted or disputed them. Rather, we are willing to discuss them as well as the Framework Document and any documents from other Parties.

As we have said before the issue or problem now is not a lack of documents. It is a lack of dialogue. We want to avoid any tactic or approach which would divert the process into a paper chase rather than a search for agreement through dialogue. We have a higher notion of peace than just building paper walls (in place of more physical ones).

We need dialogue which involves all Parties and both Governments. A dialogue that is truly inclusive and truly comprehensive because it cannot credibly be one without the other. This requires that we desist from attempts at preclusion from, or other preconditions for, dialogue.

The reality is that we have the prime condition for dialogue – the absence of violence!

We don't need any more models or blueprints at this stage. We need a table – if even that. Dialogue will not proceed without argument but it can – and must – progress to agreement.

Agreement cannot be imposed on either tradition or by either tradition. It can only be reached between them both. That is both an assurance and a challenge to each of us. It is also reflected in the Framework Document if people care to read it with reflection, rather than rejection, in mind.

We have often stressed to Unionists that we have no wish, or way, to solve this problem without them. We must also stress that we have no plot or plan to solve it against them.

In joint statements with Gerry Adams, I have made it explicit that any new democratic accord is achievable and viable only if it can earn and enjoy the allegiance of the unionist tradition as well as of the rest of us.

That is not a trap or a threat – particularly not when offered in a context where violence has ceased.

As a Forum for Peace and Reconciliation our concern must be to reach out to Unionists rather than to react to them. It is in that spirit that we speak today.

Our task is not to come to conclusions about any document (no matter how fine and fair any of us might believe it to be). It is to come to a start of real dialogue.

While we must continue with the very helpful and, at times, humbling, exercise of listening to the many diverse interests and ideas of different communities on the island, we should also start to refine the issues which will be central to the dialogue that we need.

We can be mindful that our brief in this Forum is not to negotiate or 'shadow-negotiate' remedies to all our problems. We should endeavour to offer as serious, sensitive and sympathetic assessments as possible of the key realities of our problem. We should also try to analyse from those what are essential requirements for their resolution or reconciliation.

There would be no attempt to be exclusive, and no assumptions that we can be conclusive, in that work. The aim is to engage with others not to impose on them. We would clearly be laying some things out for others and not be laying anything down for them.

The hope is that others can offer their own reflections on the realities and requirements of our situation. Because it is only by reaching a shared understanding of the problem that we can hope to arrive at an agreement on its solution.

Progress to dialogue and through dialogue will, in my view, prove the value and validity of the work that has gone into the Framework Document. I want to conclude by again thanking the dedicated officials who have worked as true public servants, not as malicious schemers, and to express the deep appreciation of the SDLP for the skill and spirit shown by both the previous and present Governments in both the preparation and presentation of the document. I want to commend, in particular, the Taoiseach for his articulation of the document's real meaning and to pay tribute to the Tanaiste for his deep personal involvement in the production of a document which is clearly intended to be helpful to all and hurtful to no traditions.

FINE GAEL

THIS IS A SIGNIFICANT MOMENT FOR THE FORUM. We now have before us a document, negotiated and agreed between two sovereign Governments. Its publication and contents have been widely welcomed and endorsed in Ireland, in Britain and by Governments in countries where there are large numbers of Irish people and people of Irish descent.

The Joint Framework Document is an unique document. It is *not* a legally binding international agreement, as the 1985 Hillsborough Agreement is. It is *not*, as the outcome of the Sunningdale Conference of 1973 was, an agreed communiqué between the Irish and British Governments and the Parties involved in the then Northern Ireland Executive. It is, simply stated, a document to assist discussion and negotiation involving the two Governments and the Northern Ireland parties. Its objectives are exactly the same as those of this Forum:

(i)   lasting peace;

(ii) stability;

(iii) reconciliation among all the people of Ireland.

It is not necessary to present the Joint Framework Document in detail. We have all had the opportunity to study it and many of us have already participated in public debate on it.

The decision which we have to take is how to integrate this document with our own work. May I suggest that, at the same time, we should also be conscious of, and take into account, the documents recently issued by both the Democratic Unionist Party and the Ulster Unionist Party.

While I share the general disappointment at the Unionist reaction to the Joint Framework Document, I take some hope from the fact that the Unionist documents — obviously containing many points with which I would disagree — were published to coincide with the Joint Framework Document. In that way, I believe that discussion has been facilitated in an important way.

I share the wish that representatives of the unionist tradition would join in our discussions, either in this Forum or elsewhere, and would add only the following message. We respect your position. We acknowledge that your identity is not ours. We recognise that your aspirations are different to ours. We want to talk to you about how, acting together and in agreement, we can accommodate our differences. Without your participation, there can be no lasting peace, no stability and no reconciliation.

John Bruton, as the Leader of Fine Gael, pointed out in his opening address to the Forum last October, that the objectives of this Forum could only be achieved if unionists join with nationalists in exploring the way forward. Not only must we review our positions and revise our thinking, but unionists must do likewise.

Following on the publication of the Joint Framework Document we in this Forum must now re-focus our work. Our predecessors in the New Ireland Forum in 1984 performed an important task, especially when they set out their understanding of what the framework for a new Ireland should be. They examined and, most importantly, agreed on what the present realities were and what the future requirements might be.

More than a decade has passed since then. There have been many positive developments. Violence has ceased. Additional Parties are now represented around this table. The two Governments have set out their agreed position. The time has, I believe, come to look again at the realities and the requirements and to see if we in this Forum can reach agreement. I hope that other Parties will give favourable consideration to this suggestion.

In conclusion, may I, on behalf of Fine Gael, convey thanks and congratulations to all who made possible the Joint Framework Document. As a group of Parties represented in this Forum, it now falls to us to take up the running. Fine Gael is ready, willing and able.

THE LABOUR PARTY

I AM DEEPLY HONOURED TO BE CALLED UPON TO OPEN THIS DEBATE in the Forum on the *New Framework for Agreement*.

This Forum, as we know, is not a negotiating forum. It has in many ways an even more important task to deepen the reserves of understanding and the store of fresh thinking which can be drawn upon by political leaders when they come to engage in comprehensive negotiations on the future of this island. I share the hope, so consistently expressed by the great majority of all shades of political opinion on the island, that these will begin sooner rather than later.

The *New Framework for Agreement* seeks to promote dialogue and reflection, not to pre-empt it. It is therefore particularly appropriate that the Forum, with its broadly similar objectives, should engage with it thoroughly and consider its implications. I have no doubt that the result will enrich further the political debate which is the necessary background to negotiations.

It is not possible, in the time available, to give a detailed overview of the document, nor is it necessary, in view of the comprehensive statements already on the record by the Taoiseach and other Government representatives. The document in any case speaks for itself.

I would like instead to concentrate on one aspect, which concerns me deeply, both personally and politically. That is the Unionist reaction to the document.

I speak as someone who, in all the long and intensive preparation that a document of this scope requires, never once knowingly lost sight of the need for unionist agreement.

I have always believed agreement between our two traditions is, quite simply, the definition of stability on this island. The notion of coercion, not to speak of violence, between our two traditions is abhorrent to me. I like to think my political career to date bears witness to that philosophy, as I intend it will do in all circumstances in the future.

When the document was published, the immediate cry was that there was nothing in it for unionists. It was denounced in the House of Commons as a capitulation to violence. We were told it exceeded the worst unionist fears.

I had always understood that the essence of unionist fears was that the nationalist majority on the island rejected the legitimacy of their position. Yet they overlook the radical new approach in the document which envisages:

... as part of a new and equitable dispensation for Northern Ireland ... recognition by both Governments of the legitimacy of whatever choice is freely exercised by a majority of the people of Northern Ireland with regard to its constitutional status, whether they prefer to continue to support the Union or a sovereign united Ireland.

This document enshrines the principle of consent more strongly than ever before. It holds out the prospect of the entire nationalist community on the island subscribing solemnly to agreed arrangements, on terms which involve no concession of basic principle for unionists.

We were told that the claims in the Irish Constitution were an outrage to unionists, and prevented the good-neighbourly relations they wished to see on the island. Unionists themselves said the 1992 talks foundered because of a lack of sufficient commitment on this issue by Irish Government negotiators. It is now no longer a semantic matter of 'could' or 'would', but an unprecedented offer of change in the clearest terms it is possible to make.

We were told that the principle of democratic accountability was crucial to unionist attitudes to a North-South body. I made sure the document fully reflected this key concern, more clearly than any previous model. I already spoke of a 'fourfold lock' to protect unionist interests in a North-South body – namely, the safeguards of unanimity, democratic accountability, clear mutual interest and reciprocity. If even further safeguards are necessary, let us hear about them.

The Irish Government was not involved in Strand One of the talks. I understand, however, the proposals in the British paper follow closely the lines of a subcommittee report of Strand One, where Unionists were not only leading participants, but bitterly reproached some Nationalists for their failure to endorse the report.

We were told that a referendum in Northern Ireland on the outcome of negotiations was a crucial and all-embracing safeguard, as indeed it seems to me to be.

These elements are all central to the document.

Is there nothing in all this for unionists?

The second theme in Unionist reaction – that the document is the fruit of violence – seems to me to miss two crucial points: The first is that there is a nationalist community in Northern Ireland with important rights which must be met, not because of violence, but even in spite of it. The notion that these rights are properly left in abeyance until violence makes it necessary to deal with them has poisoned political life and wasted great opportunity in Northern Ireland once already. I hope it will never do so again. The second point this reaction misses is that the guns are now silent. There is now an opportunity, for the first time in a generation, to address an essentially political problem in an exclusively peaceful political way. The Framework Document seeks only to give impetus and direction to this task.

I am conscious that the main Unionist Parties are absent from the Forum. I may be accused of talking at them rather than to them, but as they themselves know, it is not by choice. Their tradition prides itself on plain speaking and I hope they will not take my plain words for an absence of goodwill.

I would appeal to them to rethink their position on the document. Unionist leaders now hold in the balance not just the hopes and wishes of their own community, but those of the people of both islands.

In the United States earlier this week, I explained to a senior American politician that moderate elements in the unionist community had to look over their shoulder at the extremes. He asked me, 'Don't they have any other shoulder to look over?'

His quip contained a profound truth: over one shoulder there is the landscape of traditional unionist fears, where change must always equal defeat, and Lundy reigns supreme. Looking over the other shoulder, unionists can see a different and more promising view: they can see a nationalist community fully committed to the principle of consent and ready to contemplate a radically new relationship with unionism. They can see a determination that the goal of Irish unity will never be used as a contrivance against unionism, any more than the Union can be used as a contrivance against nationalism. They can see new arrangements which enhance the relevance and role of political leaders in Northern Ireland, not just in terms of Northern Ireland, but the wider context as well.

They can see a new relationship between these islands, where, in the words of the Framework Document

> ... the relationship between the traditions in Northern Ireland could become a positive bond of further understanding, cooperation and amity, rather than a source of contention, between the wider British and Irish democracies.

The time has come for a fundamental reappraisal of relationships between the different traditions on this island. Unionists will make a mistake of historic proportions if they abdicate their role.

Each tradition in Ireland has been profoundly affected by its historical experience. Each has proven itself, in different ways, to be indomitable. Each asserts a well-defined political identity and ethos which will never be suppressed. Each has much in its history on which it can look back with legitimate pride. Each has suffered, and also inflicted suffering. Each has felt obliged, all too frequently, to define itself in defensive and adversarial terms towards the other.

The two Governments are the inheritors of a historic responsibility to resolve this dilemma and to lay the basis for a new order of cooperation and harmony.

The Framework Document represents an attempt on our part to bridge the gap between the two traditions and to define how a new and lasting consensus might be reached, with balance and fairness towards all.

SINN FÉIN

S INN FÉIN WELCOMES THE PUBLICATION OF THE Framework Document.
Its publication should now clear the way for inclusive peace talks and
for the next phase of this process, with everyone at the table and everything
on the table. Sinn Féin will enter these peace talks on the basis of our
Republican analysis. We will put our view that a lasting peace in Ireland
can only be based on the right of all the Irish people to national self-
determination.

The Framework Document is a discussion document. It is neither a
solution nor a settlement. It does not attempt to preclude or
predetermine any particular outcome. In paragraph 8 of the document
it states 'this document is not a rigid blueprint to be imposed'. It is in
this light that we will address the Framework Document. However, its
publication by the two Governments is a clear recognition that partition
has failed and that there is no going back to the failed policies and
structures of the past.

The political framework envisaged is clearly an all-Ireland one and
even though we would like to see this more deeply rooted, prescriptive
and thoroughgoing, Sinn Féin will judge the Framework Document
pragmatically and in the context of our objectives, policy and strategy.

A lasting peace requires fundamental constitutional and political
change. Sinn Féin's objective is to bring about an inclusive and
negotiated end to British jurisdiction in Ireland. We seek to replace it

with a new and agreed Irish jurisdiction. In our view, this poses no threat to any section of our people, including the unionists.

The consent and allegiance of unionists is needed to secure a peace settlement. We want dialogue and debate with unionists to seek an agreed Ireland. We have never advocated that the Six Counties be arbitrarily absorbed into the twenty six counties. We have always argued for a new national constitution embracing the diversity of our Irishness in all of its various forms. Unionists will find that they can have more real power and control over their lives and their destiny in an agreed Ireland than they ever will as an unwanted appendage of Britain.

But unionists cannot have a veto over British policy and Mr Major and others must stop pretending that they have. The unionist leadership's desire for an internal settlement, with a devolved administration, comes from their wish to restore unionist rule, that is, unionist domination.

Change must come, and it must be change for the better. There can be no going back – partition has failed and there can be no return to a Stormont regime. Sinn Féin's attitude to Stormont is one of abstention. There can be no involvement by Republicans in any body which denies the right of the people of this island to national self-determination. Republicans will, of course, consider transitional arrangements which are linked to a clear commitment by the British Government to end British jurisdiction in our country.

One of the most significant advances of recent times is the widespread acceptance that an internal Six County settlement is not a solution. Some have come to this position because they recognise the failure of partition, and the reality that it is not only the governance of the Six Counties which has been the problem – it is the existence of the statelet itself. Others who may not share that view, or who see no other way forward have concluded also that an internal settlement is not a solution.

In their immediate reaction to the Framework Document and in their voting strategy in the British Parliament, the Unionists are once again playing the Orange Card – this time to impose a veto on the phase of inclusive negotiations which we are about to enter. Irrespective of the content of the Framework Document – of how much of it we might like or dislike – the Framework Document, and the inclusive peace talks which must now follow, should open the way for new political arrangements agreed through democratic negotiations between, and acceptable to, all the Irish people.

Sinn Féin will therefore approach these discussions on the basis that they must address all the issues at the heart of the conflict, that there can be no vetoes over these discussions and that through inclusive negotiations we can move towards a democratic agreement acceptable, for the first time, to all the Irish people.

For over two years now, Mr Major has had a minimalist approach to the peace process. Now, after the publication of the Framework Document, the strategy pursued by the British Government will indicate the extent to which they are willing to engage in advancing the peace process.

For our part, we have always maintained the centrality of inclusive dialogue, without pre-conditions, in creating the conditions for a just and lasting peace. Republicans, nationalists, unionists and loyalists are in an unique situation now, where, with a little courage and foresight, we could forge an agreed future for ourselves. Only through real peace talks, seeking agreement, can we hope to put the conflict of the past behind us. If the Framework Document succeeds in moving all of us to this point, then it will have served a useful purpose.

THE
PROGRESSIVE DEMOCRATS

TEN DAYS HAVE NOW PASSED since the publication of the Framework Document. I believe it will be seen in time as a defining moment in the evolution of the sometimes tangled, troubled and bloody relationship between Ireland and England, and between the Irish and British people who are intermixed on this island. I earnestly hope that, taken along with the Downing Street Declaration and the IRA and Loyalist ceasefires, it will provide the basis for building a lasting political settlement.

The Framework Document has correctly been presented by the two Governments not as a blueprint, but as a discussion document. But for all that, there is no disguising its fundamental importance in defining how the two Governments want these relationships to evolve.

The essential features of post-Framework Anglo-Irish and North-South relations will be:

(i)   recognition of the territorial integrity of Northern Ireland;

(ii)   consent, and not coercion, as the only basis on which the current status of Northern Ireland can be changed;

(iii)   absolute equality of rights for both unionists and nationalists within Northern Ireland; and

(iv)   the creation of strong North-South bodies, with executive powers.

This all-Ireland dimension is clearly the stumbling block for unionists. However, not only does it make economic sense, given the fact that there are just five million people on this small island, but it is also a key element in guaranteeing parity of esteem for Northern nationalists, as an expression of their Irish identity and aspirations.

Clearly this is difficult for many unionists to come to terms with. But surely they must realise that if there is to be lasting peace and true social solidarity within Northern Ireland, then the nationalist minority there must be fully reconciled with that State.

Northern Ireland, in reflecting the identity and allegiance of the unionist majority there, is partly British. But in the identity and allegiance of its nationalist community, it is also very much Irish. Furthermore, Northern Ireland already shares in a whole range of all-Ireland sporting, ecclesiastical, cultural and economic arrangements.

It has been the failure of Unionist politicians down the years to recognise these facts, and their failure to try to fully accommodate the political rights and aspirations of their nationalist fellow citizens within the State of Northern Ireland, that fed the alienation and disaffection of so many of their nationalist fellow citizens.

It is in that context that the significance of much of the Framework Document can be gauged, and in particular its statement of current British Government thinking on these issues.

I would like, for instance, to refer to the declaration by both sovereign Governments at paragraph 19 that:

> …they agree that future arrangements relating to Northern Ireland, and Northern Ireland's wider relationships should respect *the full and equal legitimacy and worth* [my emphasis] of the identity, sense of allegiance, aspiration and ethos of both the unionist and nationalist communities there.

As I have already stated in Dáil Éireann, if it appears that, in the Framework Document, nationalists in Northern Ireland have got more than unionists, that is because nationalists there have much more catching up to do.

I would appeal to unionists to ponder their status within Northern Ireland, and how it is reflected and represented, and then ask themselves how they see the Irish identity of their nationalist neighbours being vindicated.

Northern unionists have:

(i)   the Union link with Britain;

(ii)   the British administration at Stormont;

(iii)   Northern Ireland parliamentary representation at Westminster;

(iv)   the emblems of unionism, like the Union Jack.

Compared with that, what was the level of political rights, or parity of esteem accorded Northern nationalists ? Do the unionists accept that nationalists in Northern Ireland are as fully entitled to have their political rights and aspirations accommodated as they themselves?

Despite the Unionist denunciations of the Framework, I would appeal to them to realise that there are real benefits for them also.

For unionists, there is:

(i)   explicit acceptance of the principle of consent being required for any change in the current status of Northern Ireland;

(ii)   the proposed dropping of the claim of jurisdiction over Northern Ireland in the Irish Constitution;

(iii) the ultimate safeguard of a referendum by the people of Northern Ireland on any eventual settlement that emerges from all-Party talks.

I hope that such all-Party talks can soon commence. But I realise that the more realistic possibility is probably bi-lateral talks in the first instance.

I would also like to see the Irish Government having all-Party discussions in this State on the actual wording of the changes that must be made to Articles 2 and 3 of our Constitution on foot of the commitments contained in the Framework Document.

I feel that we are now at a time of great hope and optimism. We could finally be on the road to devising a lasting political settlement for Northern Ireland, between North and South, and also embracing relationships between these islands.

Despite the denunciations by so many Unionist politicians, the absence of post-Hillsborough-style street protests, and the very responsible reaction of the smaller Loyalist Parties, betokens a much more mature and sensible view on the part of the unionist community generally.

I know there are genuine fears among that community. And some of these fears are genuine. They have borne the brunt of the IRA's terrorist campaign over the past quarter of a century, when not only their menfolk in and out of uniform were murdered, but the heart was blown out of many of their towns.

That too is why the disarmament issue must be faced up to and must be one of the next steps forward. No all-Party political process can embrace participants who attend on the basis of an explicit or implicit threat that if they do not get their way they will resort to renewed terrorism.

I know that is a very real fear of the unionist community in particular. It is well grounded and it is a fear that must be addressed effectively. This will be a difficult issue to resolve. I note the comments of the Tánaiste in the United States earlier this week about involving a third party in securing the handing-in of terrorist armaments. But, however it is done, there must be tangible progress soon on this issue. I believe the political bona fides of the Republican movement are on the line in this matter.

But many difficult, and seemingly insurmountable, hurdles have already been crossed during the unfolding of the peace process. So I want to be optimistic. We simply must succeed in the task of disarmament if further significant progress is to be made in the wider political settlement process.

I also want to remember here today the victims of violence over the past twenty five years. We have already heard at first hand here at the Forum from some of the relatives of the victims, and witnessed the emotional turmoil they must endure. For the 3,000-plus victims of the Troubles there will be no brighter tomorrow, and only a lifetime of heartbreak, sadness and regret for their relatives.

The best testament we can offer to their memory is the creation of a lasting peace and the flowering of true friendship between the divided people on this island. For a long time, those aspirations appeared a forlorn hope. But the situation is not so hopeless now. In our various ways, I believe all the Parties here at the Forum, and the political representatives of the unionist community also, want to build a better future for the people of Northern Ireland; for all the people on this island, and for our friends and neighbours in Britain. Let us hope that we succeed.

THE ALLIANCE PARTY

SINCE THE ANGLO–IRISH AGREEMENT OF 1985, one of the great frustrations in our attempts to make progress towards a settlement has been the failure of the two Governments to produce their own proposals. I first called in 1989 for the British Government to put its proposals for the future government of Northern Ireland down on paper for consultation, and I have repeated this call both publicly and privately on many occasions since. During the Inter-Party Talks in 1991 and 1992 my frustration became a shared view amongst many of the political Party representatives, and since the end of the formal talks process in late 1992 pressure continued to mount for a clear statement of the Governmental view on the possible shape of a settlement involving all three sets of relationships outlined as the basis for talks in March 1991.

I welcome therefore the publication of the two Framework Documents, not because I agree with all that is there, any more than I agreed with the presentations of the UUP, the SDLP or the DUP during the talks. I welcome the documents as a very significant contribution to the peace process and I and my colleagues are prepared to continue our discussions with both Governments, and *all* the other political Parties, informed by the proposals described in the Framework papers. As I have repeatedly said in the last two weeks, these papers are a basis for negotiation not a basis for hysteria or alarm.

This is not a time to deal in particular detail with very complex proposals, but I would take this opportunity to describe how the

Alliance approach to the development of a settlement will continue to depend on our measurement of all proposals against a number of principles.

As our very name, Alliance, makes clear, we will want to ensure that all sides in our community have their rights recognised and respected. In the future, power must never be exercised exclusively by one or other side in favour of their own. Power and responsibility must now be exercised across the divisions in our community, and in the best interests of *all* our people. There are, however, three other principles which inform our judgements.

Firstly, *participation*. Does what is proposed give an opportunity for the people of Northern Ireland to be involved in their own governance? In every community the involvement of the people is a moral right and a practical requirement if there is to be stability, allegiance to and acceptance of the organs of state. One of the great weaknesses of the Anglo-Irish Agreement was the flimsy way in which this principle was observed. The strength of the Framework proposals lies in the opportunities that are offered for the development of participatory democracy. The establishment of an Assembly, representative North-South structures, a democratising input to the Anglo-Irish Conference, and a North-South Inter-Parliamentary body are some of the most important ways in which the principle of participation is upheld in these proposals, and this we welcome.

The second principle is *accountability*. This requires that the governed are not only involved but empowered. The most striking example of this is the assertion in the documents that it will be for the people of Northern Ireland to decide their own constitutional future. The entrenchment of this principle in current political vocabulary has certainly made rational discussion about the political future much more possible in Northern Ireland. The principle of accountability also moves us away from appointed bodies towards elected bodies, from arms-length centralism to subsidiarity and, in the case of cross-border relations, it requires that any North-South structure is subordinate and accountable to the assembly in the North, and the Oireachtas in the South, rather than the reverse. The imperative of accountability is not negotiable. If fully implemented it may resolve other problems. If, for example, policing in Northern Ireland was directly accountable to a power-sharing assembly, instead of to Westminster, many of the deepest difficulties in this contentious area might begin to become soluble.

The third touchstone which we use is that of *transparency*. This Forum is making a very useful contribution to the peace process because it is open and transparent. Its transparency would be greatly assisted if the media in Northern Ireland were as attentive to our proceedings as their colleagues in this jurisdiction. It is important that our people can see what is going on in their name. Any sense that proceedings are going on in secret and behind closed doors always excites anxiety, and in our divided community that does not mean anticipatory anxiety, but rather paranoid anxiety.

In South Africa transparency has become a watchword of reform, and so it must also be for us. The essence of transparency is simplicity. Unnecessary complexity is often merely a technique for obfuscation. If there is to be openness and constructive debate, the complexity of this document and its proposals must be overcome. People can understand the need for free and fair elections, a proportionate assembly and power-sharing government, but they regard with understandable suspicion the proposal for a panel with curious and uncertain powers and procedures. Northern Irish people understand the value of cross-border cooperation, of Ministers from both sides meeting to find new ways of working together, but they become suspicious of more grandiose schemes with unclear parameters, especially when some rudimentary cooperative ventures are neglected.

Finally, I myself am suspicious when a simple commitment to a Bill of Rights justiciable through our own courts is replaced by paragraphs of meaningless high-sounding diplomacy. Let us have a clear commitment to a Bill of Rights, and of course also to changes in Articles 2 and 3 and, if it is of help, let us entrench the principle of consent in the Government of Ireland Act. Clarity is the enemy of suspicion and of those who work by deceit.

I believe that the overwhelming majority of people in Northern Ireland want us to talk. I am at this Forum because people want their views to be represented. Gone are the days when they were content to let them go by default. I do not claim to represent unionists but many unionist people have contacted me to ask that I take their views into account when I am participating in this Forum, so that they are not left entirely without a voice where it matters. The people want peace, and after six months of ceasefire they are determined not to return to the nightmare. People are beginning to believe that a stable peace and an honourable settlement is possible. This is a very important development, and one which no one can ignore. We must talk about the future together and I would appeal to the leaders of unionism and loyalism not to allow their fears to deprive them of the opportunity to participate in building a new future. The people are demanding that we negotiate our way forward.

DEMOCRATIC LEFT

THE MANNER IN WHICH THE Joint Framework Document is interpreted in Ireland over the next few weeks will determine whether meaningful talks will take place within the parameters it sets out.

The document is balanced, but the balance is seen by many as being tilted towards nationalism. Accordingly, it has united elements of both unionism and nationalism who see it as blueprint for a united Ireland.

Nationalists will claim that this is their due and merely redresses the balance that obtained during fifty years of unionist rule.

However, this is to miss the point. As Proinsias De Rossa pointed out in Dáil Éireann:

> This document is an enabling document not a straight-jacket. It says to the political Parties of Northern Ireland that it is possible to resolve the problems of Northern Ireland in an exclusively peaceful and democratic way and a way perceived to be fair by all the people of that society. But it addresses itself to those political Parties by saying people must participate in this decision-making. Not to do so, whether through attachment to an absolutist position which accommodates violence as a means to an end; or through an unwillingness, bordering on unreason, to recognise that Northern Ireland is a very singular place 'more British than the British, more Irish than the Irish' is a failure of

judgement and of nerve and is certainly a failure to show leadership. What this document guarantees is that nobody in Northern Ireland will be less British and nobody will be less Irish.

This last point is crucial. The Framework Document does not deny the national allegiance of anybody in Northern Ireland. It recognises the rights of all and fully endorses equality of citizenship. And it accepts the rights of self-determination by the people of Northern Ireland. Yet the document is unacceptable to the major Unionist Parties. They see it as a threat to the Union and feel excluded from the future it envisages. They feel betrayed and isolated.

Unionist discomfort has been a cause of satisfaction in some nationalist circles. President Robinson cautions us all to note that:

We have to build trust. We have to listen to, understand and respect, respect the fears. When fears are as genuine and deep-rooted as that, if we don't respect them, we have not understood. The fear is very genuine. The fear of the ground shifting, the fear of a takeover, is undermining a sense of security.

Understanding is an essential precondition of reconciliation. Likewise, reconciliation involves both a recognition and an acceptance of difference. And nationalist and unionist differences are deeply rooted in history and have been reinforced by twenty five years of violence.

These differences won't disappear at the drop of a constitutional claim. Neither will 300 years of grievance be overturned by the legal recognition of nationalism in Northern Ireland. But such steps will help build security and confidence among all the people of Northern Ireland. This in turn will facilitate agreement within Northern Ireland, and between Northern Ireland and the Republic.

This will take time and will require patience. The 'long war' is still fresh in the memory of those who were the target of a sustained terrorist campaign. Others have suffered at the hands of both agents and 'defenders' of the State. Now that the paramilitary campaigns have been suspended, it is easy to see the futility of political violence. It is another thing to complete the journey from fragile ceasefires to a permanent peace and to agreement between all Parties.

The cause of peace is badly served by claims that victory is in sight and that a united Ireland in around the corner. A policy of 'compulsory Irishness' is doomed to failure. This is a purely territorial concept that takes no account of the conflicting, but legitimate, political allegiances of the people of Northern Ireland.

Unfortunately, the Joint Framework Document is also weak on this score. The constant references to 'two communities' ignore the reality of a growing secularist, pluralist tendency in Northern Ireland that does not subscribe to the old loyalties and is not bound by the old prejudices. This emerging 'third strand' will be crucial to arriving at an agreement and must be fully engaged in the search for a settlement.

Little attention has been paid to the British Government's Framework for Accountable Government in Northern Ireland. The lack of any stated commitment to a Bill of Rights is a grave disappointment. Democratic Left have argued for a Bill of Rights that would meet the concerns of all sections of the community. A new constitutional framework for Northern Ireland must contain cast-iron legal protection of communal and individual rights.

The proposal of a panel, which has already been dubbed 'The Three Wise Men', could give rise to problems in that it has the potential to further institutionalise sectarianism. This is to be avoided at all costs.

Sections of the internal document are said to build on areas of agreement reached in 1992, in which case the DUP should be on board. But what of Sinn Féin? The Party's attitude to participation in a Northern Ireland assembly is ambiguous to say the least. A democratic mandate carries with it responsibilities as well as rights and these will not be met by abstentionism.

Similarly, something other than abstentionism is called for from the Unionist Parties. As a contributor to the current issue of *Fortnight* who was involved in brokering the Loyalist ceasefire writes:

'Ulster Says No' can not forever ignore the fact that at least forty percent say yes. If unionism is to be properly represented, the onus is on the UUP and the Democratic Unionists to recognise this, and to respond to the challenge of the Framework Document – by entering talks with the representatives of this forty percent. Anything less would be a denial of reality and, once again, an abdication of responsibility fully to represent the views of those who elected them.

Unionists should note that seventy nine percent of Protestants in Northern Ireland say that Unionist Parties should take part in talks based upon the document. Likewise, the Nationalist Parties, North and South, should note that a substantial majority in the Republic backs reform of Articles 2 and 3. And an overwhelming majority says it's time for the paramilitaries to give up their guns.

The people are giving a lead that the politicians would be foolish to ignore. Politicians in the Republic are ill-advised to play to the gallery on Articles 2 and 3; reconciliation, like harmonisation, cuts both ways. All of us, as political representatives, should acknowledge and respect the views and aspirations of those with whom we differ. When we talk about change, we must accept that it means change for all of us and be prepared to live up to the challenge that implies.

For these reasons, political leaders in the Republic must disavow any triumphalist reading of the Framework Document. Last week's remarks about 'A Nation Once Again' by the leader of the main opposition Party in the Republic reflect an insular and exclusive nationalism which echoed the previous leaders' dogmatic assertion of 'the one nation theory'. Such remarks only serve to fuel unionist fears not alone about Fianna Fáil intentions but about the ambitions of the Framework Document.

If the document contains any aspects which are threatening or triumphalist, or which are so constructed, then it is up to political leaders in the Republic to empty them of any such content. There is a protracted period of negotiation ahead and, if agreement is to be reached, Parties in the Republic must play a cooperative and constructive role, informed by wisdom and sensitivity.

SENATOR GORDON WILSON

PEOPLE REFER TO THIS AS A 'Framework Document' and we have done so all afternoon. The copy I have says that it is *A New Framework for Agreement,* and I think that the last two words are very significant. It is a complex document. Not everyone does, or maybe will, understand it. I am not sure that I fully understand it, but I want to take it as a whole and not just pull out the pieces of which I might not be so sure. It is a framework. It is not being imposed. There are guarantees built into it for everyone. It is a basis for thought and discussion. It calls for consent, for trust, for respect and, in my view, it is a giant step on the way to peace. I welcome it and I support it.

It seems to me it is the best opportunity for peace that we have had after twenty five years when 3,000 people lost their lives, and when in the last six months only one person has lost his life. I turn on my radio in the morning without the fear that I am going to hear of another death, or another bomb, and that message seems to be getting through to the people, especially to those who live in Northern Ireland. People want and yearn and long and pray for peace, and I think the atmosphere is right and ripe for a settlement. It is time for change. This will not be easy. Northern Ireland never is. But I have hope.

I have to say that I am saddened, for want of a better word, by the response from Unionist politicians to the document. I can understand their doubts because they do feel exposed and isolated and unloved, but I get a little cross when I hear them use words like 'sell-out', 'insult', 'betrayal'. These are strong words. And I get more than a little cross when I see David Trimble being melodramatic on television. And I got very cross indeed when my MP, Ken Maginnis, talked in the House of Commons about the document putting us back ten years. I cannot believe that Ken Maginnis wants to go back to ten years ago and to the murders and the bombs. I would say this to the Unionists, not in anger, and certainly not to lecture them – that is not my job – but I would say it in love and charity: 1690 was over three centuries ago; we are heading for the twenty first century. Time has moved on.

I appeal above all to them to stop playing politics with people's lives, to look over their shoulder and to listen to what their grass-roots supporters are saying. I made it my business to meet as many people from my community as I possibly could in the two days of the last ten which I have spent in Enniskillen. They said that they want their political leaders to talk. The least supportive comment I heard about the document came from someone who would be fairly described as a hard line unionist and who said that perhaps the document was 'a little too green'.

It seems to me that the unionist man and woman in the street are prepared to compromise. Compromise is not giving in; it is maturity. I appeal to the political leaders to sit down, all of them, to listen to their electors, to present their policies, to reach out to love their neighbours and their common God, and so to help us towards achieving peace, a lasting peace, because I think that is what this document is about.

THE GREEN PARTY

WE WELCOME THE PUBLICATION OF THE Framework Document which offers a rough outline of what a compromise in the Northern Ireland context might look like. From a Green Party perspective, whilst there are many details with which we might take issue, we wish to make clear our support for the general direction that the document takes. Ours is a radically decentralist policy, favouring non-adversarial models of political organisation and decision-making which would transform any democratic society from divisive nation statism to a more cohesive grass-roots-based democracy. This has particular implications for our approach to the Northern Ireland conflict. The Framework Document makes clear what the depth of a true compromise in the Northern Ireland situation will be. We particularly welcome the stress upon a balanced constitutional adjustment and, for the first time that we are aware of in a formal government document, there is an acceptance of the need to construct a 'political consensus'. This has been a cornerstone of Green policy since our foundation and, whilst we feel that the document at times runs counter to the requirements of consensus, particularly in regard to its commitment to the majoritarian principle on the constitutional status of Northern Ireland, we do feel that by formally taking on the language of consensus the Governments have taken an important step forward.

Turning to the text of the document, we welcome the realisation in paragraph 44 that the issue of policing is intertwined with the issue of political consensus, and the necessity for new institutions with community identification.

Whilst reiterating our clear support for the general direction that this document takes, we would urge caution when designing systems to give effect to the critical principle of 'parity of esteem'. There is no mention of gender balancing, an issue which should be addressed. Regarding the approach to power-sharing in the assembly, we suggest that the principle of proportionality should apply, not only to any elected posts, but also to the decision-making. Senator John Robb has in the past suggested the use of the matrix vote for the election of office bearers, and this is a suggestion to which we would urge the Government Parties to give serious consideration. Care should be taken not to institutionalise the divide nor to disenfranchise those who do not identify primarily with either tradition. Furthermore, we would argue that if the two Governments reject the use of a simple majority on all controversial issues in the assembly, it is absolutely vital for them to reject that same simple majority vote on the most controversial issue of all – the constitutional status.

Regarding the proposal for a three person panel, we would suggest it be increased to five in order to grant it greater representative capacity and would further suggest its role be largely seen as 'referee' to the assembly, acting as a facilitator of, rather than contributor to, debate.

We recognise the misgivings of the Unionist Parties. However, this document represents the most significant development in Anglo-Irish relations since 1992. It is vital that all parties engage in talks now. No Party has any right to exclude any other by threats or boycotts. This conflict cannot be resolved without compromise and the Framework Document offers a form of draft compromise. The absolute positions of both Unionism and Nationalism must, by definition, be modified if a compromise is to emerge. The best place now for the Unionist Parties is around the table where the actual form of compromise will be decided.

INDEPENDENT DEPUTIES IN DÁIL ÉIREANN

I WILL TRY AS QUICKLY AS I CAN to run through what is my view of the Framework Document. It talks about balance. I do not think it is balanced and I do not think that it is unbalanced, in so far as the Unionists are concerned, far from it.

I think it's time that we looked at the situation and asked ourselves whether or not the Unionists now or in the future wish to have any accommodation of a peaceful nature with the rest of this island. I think it's time to call a spade a spade and I believe that the Unionists have not changed, and I don't mean the general body of people so described, but rather their leaders, not only now but back in the 1920s and back in 1912, when with guns and the threat of guns they succeeded, with the collusion of some of the British establishment, in blackmailing the British into bringing about the sorry plight that has been our lot, as a result of the partition of our country for the last seventy five years.

Now, it is not guns or the threat of guns, although some spokesmen for some of the Unionists have talked about war in the near future. I am not taking that terribly seriously, but the crying and whinging that has been going on for these months past has, I have no doubt, had a bearing on the content of the Framework Document, which is so favourable to those extreme Unionists that if they had the writing of it themselves I doubt they could have come up with anything better.

I think that the political blackmail attempts on John Major should be seen for what they are. They are really a repetition of other blackmail efforts in the past. Remember the Sunningdale Agreement? I didn't agree with it, but that's neither here nor there. But it was not acceptable to the said Unionist leaders of that time. The Anglo-Irish Agreement again was not acceptable to them and certainly not acceptable to me. It was, as the then leader of Fianna Fáil said, copperfastening partition. And power-sharing failed, again because of the intransigence of the same Unionist leadership.

The Downing Street Declaration is unacceptable to those same leaders of the Unionist people, despite the veto built in to keep the British in occupation to Tibb's Eve. Is that in fact a reasonable approach from those who regrettably have failed to turn up to any of our discussions here and don't seem likely to do so in the foreseeable future?

As the Framework Document is unacceptable to them, what I am asking them and challenging them to say is, what do you, the leaders of the main Unionist Parties, want? Would you tell us what it is and then perhaps in our discussions – which I applaud and am delighted to be part of, meeting people I might otherwise never have met – can we not have your demands straight on the table and let you come here and talk with us about them? Instead, we have the Forum being discussed by the Unionists. All one can say is — and I speak as a Donegal man and an Ulster man, a child of partition, a child of the Civil War, the son of an IRA man and a Cumman na mBan mother, and a person who was reared on Fianna Fáil until I parted ways with them, or they parted with me — I do not believe there can or ever will be real peace in this country until we are on the road to an undivided country and people. And I say to those in the Unionist fraternity that Section 75 of the Ireland Act must be on the table if ever Articles 2 and 3 are to be. I am puzzled because of the mention of both the Constitution and the 1920 Act. There is no accident about the mention of Articles 2 and 3 and the Government of Ireland Act from both the British and the Irish Government. I wish to say that unless both are on the table together there can be no resolution of either. There can be no agreement, I hope, by the people South of the border to change Articles 2 and 3 without 75 being dealt with as well.

The six border counties, of which mine is one, have only of late been given any recognition as having a part to play, or having had any deprivation, over the years since partition. I am glad it's now recognised but it is recognised as an aside rather than as part and parcel of the entire situation. It is a dangerous myth to have peace at any price. Too high a price and you wouldn't have peace. You may have it for tomorrow, next year and the year after, but you won't have it for long. That is not what we are about. We are trying to get peace for all of our time, now and the future.

We are bending over backwards to assure the unionists that they have nothing to fear, and there is little bending anyway to assure the nationalists either North or South that they have anything to be glad of, or to be satisfied with. We are not balanced in our approach, and I say in all seriousness that the unilateral decommissioning of arms, which has been put up as a block to the discussions with Sinn Féin, would be a serious mistake. Do we want to find ourselves back in 1969 again when there was nobody had arms of any kind to protect the nationalists who were under siege? Do we want to return to that? When there is decommissioning let it be broad, let it be universal, and let the arms of the 150,000 licensed gun holders, ninety percent of which are unionists, be called in. Let's keep in mind the partisan police force. Let's keep in mind the remnants of the B-Specials, who ultimately became the Ulster Defence Regiment, and the remnants of which are now in the RIR, The Royal Irish Regiment. That is where we go if we decommission unilaterally. Don't do it unless you want a repetition of 1969.

And might I say that what has been going on in Armagh in the last few weeks is inconceivable. The saturation of South Armagh, and what has been going on in Derry over the last week are incredible, and prompt me to ask is this a provocation to break the IRA ceasefire? If it is, it is not happening. But even to add to that, what do we find in the last couple of days in Westminster but a renewal of the Prevention of Terrorism Act under which over the years ninety percent of those held were Irish, or of Irish extraction, of those, ninety percent were freed without charge after seven days and yet it's going to be renewed against the background of ceasefire from the paramilitaries on both sides. What is going on in Westminster and who in fact is prompting this provocation?

Let me say as well, that in the last few days I have found it annoying and provocative that visitors from this country going to visit political prisoners in Britain, having cleared the lines, got their dates fixed, time of visit and all the rest, arrive at the prison to find that the prisoner has been moved. This is an old dodge that went on for twenty odd years. It is still going on.

INDEPENDENT SENATORS

THE FRAMEWORK DOCUMENT DESERVES support as a constructive and imaginative contribution towards the civilised solution of a 400 year old problem. I intend no discourtesy to those who have laboured so devotedly, and so fruitfully, to arrive at this stage in the search for a solution, if I suggest that it seems to contain one fundamental contradiction in principle, which we must continue to strive to resolve.

The Taoiseach told the Dáil that:

> …It is the beginning of work towards a wholly new form of expression of traditional aspirations, focusing on individuals and communities rather than on territory. By expressing aspirations in this new way, we hope that the two otherwise irreconcilable sets of aspirations can, in fact, be reconciled.

I believe this approach is central to a just and lasting solution. But operationalising it is very difficult. In particular, what are its implications for our approach towards amending Bunreacht na hÉireann? Paragraph 21 of the Framework Document commits us to change the Constitution solely on the basis of territorial criteria. We are to abandon the territorial claim until a majority of the people of Northern Ireland accept it, in which case, according to paragraph 17, 'the two Governments will introduce and support legislation to give effect to that wish'. But this clings to a fifty per cent plus one concept of democracy on a purely territorial basis. In principle, it would make much more 'democratic' sense to simply redraw the border. I am not proposing that, because it would create as many new practical problems as it would solve. But the argument in its favour is irrefutable on the basis of the very principles invoked in the Framework Document.

Is it not curious that the Document strives to assert the primacy of people within territory, in that every proposal for internal arrangements within Northern Ireland recognises that genuine democracy demands that a majority of both traditions agree on policies, but on the more fundamental issue of the existence of the State, the Document reverts to the territorial principle? I believe that our Constitution should state unequivocally that we have no aspiration, as a matter of principle, to rule anybody against their will, whatever the numbers game may turn out to be in some hypothetical future.

This is not because I suffer from any inferiority complex about either the philosophy or the record of Irish nationalism historically. It is true that there have been sordid things done in its name. Only political expediency, however, would enable one subscribe to the convenient but fraudulent historical revisionism which seeks to assert that the line of the border was created on the basis of some sort of democratic mandate. It was not. The precise line of the border was imposed by military power. But to seek to impose on unionists the principle of majoritarian rule on which they have sought to justify their control of nationalist areas would simply be to invoke their own principles against themselves. It would be the other side of what has now become the tarnished coin, indeed the counterfeit coin, of majoritarian democracy in a situation of conflicting identities.

Irish nationalism must move beyond that type of thinking, however cathartic the process may be for us. I am not one of those who believe that the way to cherish both traditions equally is to abandon both equally. We should not descend to animal level by erasing any sense of a past. We can continue to take pride in our past, but we must simultaneously transcend it.

The Taoiseach, Mr Bruton, insisted that we could not negotiate our Constitution with Britain, that that was a matter solely for our sovereign selves. I hope many would agree, however, that we should seek to discuss it with not only Northern nationalists but Northern unionists. If we are to assert any aspiration to a united Ireland, even on the principles of the Framework Document, in however hypothetical a future, are they not entitled to be consulted about the form in which we cast our aspirations? We should listen to them, and not proceed unilaterally with any amendment to the Articles we instituted unilaterally, for understandable historical reasons, in 1937.

I believe we should go beyond that – and as a modest index of how flexible Southern thinking on the North can be, I have changed my own views somewhat since speaking on the Framework Document in the Seanad two days ago. Of course the final decision on our Constitution should be made by ourselves. But if the British are to amend the Government of Ireland Act, as suggested in paragraph 20, why should not the two Governments find a further shared understanding of the Northern situation on the basis of the primacy of identities and peoples rather than territory? Why should *not* both Governments revise these documents by asserting that they do not claim in *principle* the right to rule over those people in Northern Ireland who wish to belong to another jurisdiction, that they may rule as a matter of practical convenience, but not as a matter of legitimacy over people who reject that legitimacy.

This is the only criterion on which a genuine principle of democratic self-determination can be based, the only criterion on which genuine parity of esteem can be based – the principle that neither London nor Dublin seek, as a matter of right, jurisdiction over those who do not wish to be part of their jurisdiction. It is only on that principle that the problem can be reconceptualised in terms of people rather than territory. I see no reason why both Governments could not adopt that approach on the basis of the principles they themselves proclaim in the Framework Document.

This may all seem highly abstract to practical people, or those who like to think of themselves as practical people. There are answers to that. Firstly, if we are to revise our own Constitution to reflect a more inclusive concept of Irishness that ought to be on the basis of a concept of democracy less debatable than that used in the Framework Document. The idea of democracy in that document is highly vulnerable to criticism. I won't express these possible criticisms here, but I, for one, would voice them most vigorously in a referendum campaign. Whether we like it or not, we are dealing with matters of fundamental principle, and not only of practical convenience. There will not be a lasting peace unless that peace is based on just principles.

If 'practical people' could have solved this problem, it would have been solved long ago. There was never a more practical politician, a more adept deal maker, than David Lloyd George. I do not invoke Lloyd George's name in order to denounce him. He has been unjustifiably demonised in the Irish pantheon of villains. But his 'practical' solution did not solve the problem because it was based on opportunism rather than principle. It would be tragic if the same fate were to befall this imaginative, ingenious and well-intentioned document. Instead of recoiling from practical difficulties, we have to think through how to resolve them once we get the principles right. I believe that it is only by fully exploring the implications of the proposition that territory should be defined in terms of people rather than people in terms of territory that we will irreversibly advance the search for a just and, therefore, lasting peace.

I also believe that this would be consonant with the finer, as distinct from the baser, principles of the Irish nationalist tradition.

THE WORKERS' PARTY

FOR MANY YEARS NOW THE WORKERS' PARTY have consistently
argued that the two sovereign Governments must bring out their own
views and proposals on a possible way forward for Northern Ireland. This
was not because we wished to by-pass or go over the heads of the people,
or the elected representatives, or the political Parties in Northern Ireland,
for that would be a negation of democracy, but because we believe that
the two Governments are not mere observers in this matter. As sovereign
Governments they have a responsibility to play a leading role in
facilitating a workable political agreement for the people of Northern
Ireland, and indeed for all of the people on this land. Therefore we
welcome the fact that they have published their framework proposals.

Like most other people, we have not yet reached a conclusive position
on the many important and detailed matters contained within these
proposals, and it might not even be desirable, as others have mentioned,
to go into them in detail at this stage, but we would like to make some
initial contribution.

Firstly, we welcome the fact that the document has been made widely
available, and is presented for discussion with a view to winning the
approval of the people of Northern Ireland and their political
representatives. If nothing else this would appear to acknowledge the
disastrous experience of the Anglo-Irish Agreement's publication, and
recognise that, no matter how well-intentioned, any proposals that are

foisted upon the people of Northern Ireland against their wishes simply will not work.

As John Alderdice of the Alliance Party mentioned, one of the other great benefits of having the proposals widely available amongst the public, is, I believe, the fact that it has gone a long way towards preventing the street disturbances which followed the Anglo-Irish Agreement's publication.

And, secondly, notwithstanding the fact that the proposals do indeed carry the moral authority of both Governments, we welcome the fact that the framework proposals are not considered to be the final say or the only possible proposals. Others in Northern Ireland may have ideas of their own. The DUP and UUP have both presented proposals last week. They, too, should be on the table for discussion, for what is important is that we create the conditions where it is possible for all Parties in Northern Ireland to be at the conference table. In that respect I would welcome the very generous comments that have been made by earlier speakers in relation to this matter, because certainly the message I received from unionist people, particularly, but not exclusively, from working class communities, was the fact that the way should be left open for all Parties within Northern Ireland to have the opportunity to come to the conference table. And I believe that is the express wish of all the political Parties within Northern Ireland.

Thirdly, The Workers' Party welcome the emphasis in the proposals on winning the consent of both the people of Northern Ireland and the political Parties to any future agreement. In particular, we welcome the statement now shared by almost all the political Parties on this island, that there can be no change in the constitutional status of Northern Ireland without the consent of the majority of the people there.

Fourthly, we are pleased that there appears to be a recognition of the necessity for a Bill of Rights, not only in Northern Ireland but on the island as a whole. A strong and entrenched Bill of Rights is central to winning confidence for any future administration within Northern Ireland. We have long argued that it has an equally important role on this part of the island as well. Whilst we acknowledge the British Government's constitutional difficulty on this matter, we hope that it can be overcome without diluting the scope and content of matters covered by a Bill of Rights.

I note that previous speakers perhaps felt that the commitment to a Bill of Rights may not have been as explicit as it could have been, but I note that the Secretary of State for Northern Ireland on television last Sunday, did refer directly to a Bill of Rights.

Fifthly, we welcome the proposal to establish an assembly in Northern Ireland which would contain the potential to develop significant powers in areas such as the economy, health and education and so on. The more power and influence the people of Northern Ireland can exercise over their own affairs, will be a real test of the extent and the value of democracy in Northern Ireland. However, we are concerned by the proposal to establish, whether by election or not, a panel of three, 'the Three Wise Men' as they are already being called in Northern Ireland, which would in practice oversee and manage the running of the assembly. This, in our view, would put the panel in unnecessary conflict with a democratically elected assembly.

What Northern Ireland needs most is the opening up of political life, the development of a real and participative democratic culture. It is almost impossible to conceive that the election of this three person panel would reflect anything more than the sterile, rigid and sectarian divisions within Northern Ireland. If the purpose of this panel is to provide a mechanism to guard against the abuse of power by an assembly then we would suggest that this purpose would be better served by a constitutional court which we have proposed in our submission on a Bill of Rights,

The Workers' Party equally acknowledge the value and importance to both parts of the island of meaningful cooperation on a North-South basis. However, such cooperation must be structured and operated in a way which has the support and confidence of all. It cannot be successful otherwise. We would wish to look further at the proposals in these areas before making more detailed comment.

Finally Chairperson, whilst we acknowledge the importance of constitutional, legislative and structural measures, we would point out that these alone cannot, and will not, overcome the sectarian divisions in our community which are at the root of the problem. Sectarian values and attitudes, prejudice and intolerance can only be eradicated when there is a change in the practices and culture of our public life. Therefore, alongside structural reforms, there is a need for a range of measures which in practice will forge greater unity amongst people.

In conclusion, Chairperson, the people of Northern Ireland have suffered greatly indeed over this last number of years, but more recent history has been a time of relief and great hope that a new way forward is possible. Therefore all political leaders have a responsibility to take up those opportunities, but let us not underestimate the many political bridges still to be crossed and fears yet to be soothed, but at least let us begin that task

FORUM FOR PEACE AND
RECONCILIATION

TERMS OF REFERENCE

THE FORUM FOR PEACE AND RECONCILIATION is being established
by the Government in accordance with their intentions as
expressed in the Joint Declaration, for as long as is necessary, to consult
on and examine ways in which lasting peace, stability and reconciliation
can be established by agreement among all the people of Ireland, and on
the steps required to remove barriers of distrust, on the basis of
promoting respect for the equal rights and validity of both traditions and
identities. It will also explore ways in which new approaches can be
developed to serve economic interests common to both parts of Ireland,
including in the framework of European Union. It will be a
fundamental guiding principle of the Forum and of participation in it
that all differences relating to the exercise of the right of self-
determination of the people of Ireland, and to all other matters, will be
resolved exclusively by peaceful and democratic means. The purpose of
the Forum will be to provide, as far as possible, an opportunity to both
major traditions as well as to others, to assist in identifying and clarifying
issues which could most contribute to creating a new era of trust and
cooperation on the island. Participation in the Forum will be entirely
without prejudice to the position on constitutional issues held by any
Party.

LIST OF SPEAKERS

PAPERS ON
THE NATURE OF THE PROBLEM AND THE PRINCIPLES UNDERLYING ITS RESOLUTION

1. FIANNA FÁIL paper delivered on 18 November 1994 by **Mr Albert Reynolds** TD

2. SOCIAL DEMOCRATIC AND LABOUR PARTY paper delivered on 18 November 1994 by **Mr Eddie McGrady** MP

3. FINE GAEL paper delivered on 25 November 1994 by **Mr Austin Currie** TD

4. LABOUR PARTY paper delivered on 2 December 1994 by **Mr Dick Spring** TD

5. SINN FÉIN paper delivered on 25 November 1994 by **Mr Pat Doherty**

6. PROGRESSIVE DEMOCRATS paper delivered on 9 December 1994 by **Ms Mary Harney** TD

7. ALLIANCE PARTY paper delivered on 9 December 1994 by **Dr John Alderdice**

8. DEMOCRATIC LEFT paper delivered on 2 December 1994 by **Mr Proinsias de Rossa** TD

9. Paper delivered on 13 January 1995 by **Senator Gordon Wilson**

10. THE GREEN PARTY/AN COMHAONTAS GLAS paper delivered on 13 January 1995 by **Mr Trevor Sargent** TD

11. Paper delivered on behalf of the INDEPENDENT DEPUTIES on 27 January 1995 by **Mr Neil Blaney** TD

12. Paper delivered on behalf of the INDEPENDENT SENATORS on 27 January 1995 by **Senator Joe O'Toole**

13. THE WORKERS' PARTY paper delivered on 27 January 1995 by **Mr John Lowry**

Continued overleaf

RESPONSES TO
A NEW FRAMEWORK FOR AGREEMENT
DELIVERED ON

3 MARCH 1995

1. **Ms Mary O'Rourke TD** on behalf of FIANNA FÁIL
2. **Mr John Hume MP, MEP** on behalf of the SOCIAL DEMOCRATIC AND LABOUR PARTY
3. **Mr Austin Currie TD** on behalf of FINE GAEL
4. **Mr Dick Spring TD** on behalf of the LABOUR PARTY
5. **Ms Lucilita Breathnach** on behalf of SINN FÉIN
6. **Ms Mary Harney TD** on behalf of the PROGRESSIVE DEMOCRATS
7. **Dr John Alderdice** on behalf of the ALLIANCE PARTY
8. **Mr Seamus Lynch** on behalf of DEMOCRATIC LEFT
9. **Senator Gordon Wilson**
10. **Mr Trevor Sargent TD** on behalf of the GREEN PARTY/AN COMHAONTAS GLAS
11. **Mr Neil Blaney TD** on behalf of the INDEPENDENT DEPUTIES
12. **Senator Joseph Lee** on behalf of the INDEPENDENT SENATORS
13. **Mr John Lowry** on behalf of THE WORKERS' PARTY